OXFORD MEDIEVAL TEXTS

General Editors

D. E. GREENWAY   B. F. HARVEY
M. LAPIDGE

THE WALTHAM CHRONICLE

THE
WALTHAM CHRONICLE

*An account of the discovery of
our holy cross at Montacute and
its conveyance to Waltham*

EDITED AND TRANSLATED BY

LESLIE WATKISS

and

MARJORIE CHIBNALL

CLARENDON PRESS · OXFORD

1994

Oxford University Press, Walton Street, Oxford OX2 6DP
Oxford New York Toronto
Delhi Bombay Calcutta Madras Karachi
Kuala Lumpur Singapore Hong Kong Tokyo
Nairobi Dar es Salaam Cape Town
Melbourne Auckland Madrid
and associated companies in
Berlin Ibadan

Oxford is a trade mark of Oxford University Press

Published in the United States
by Oxford University Press Inc., New York

British Library Cataloguing in Publication Data
Data available

Library of Congress Cataloging in Publication Data
Data available
ISBN 0– 19– 822164– 9

1 3 5 7 9 10 8 6 4 2

Typeset by Joshua Associates Ltd., Oxford
Printed in Great Britain
on acid-free paper by
Biddles Ltd.,
Guildford and King's Lynn

PREFACE

THIS edition might never have seen the light of day but for the enthusiasm and initial help of Dr Kenneth Bascombe of the Waltham Abbey Historical Society and of Dr Stephen Doree, who for different reasons were urging that a modern edition of the Waltham Chronicle be undertaken. Initially LW embarked on the project alone; but Professor Henry Loyn suggested the submission of the early material to the editors of the Oxford Medieval Texts, and at this stage MC was invited to collaborate in the edition. The groundwork for the text and translation had already been completed by LW; the greater part of the Introduction, except for the section on the manuscripts has been provided by MC; both have collaborated fully in the revision and rewriting of the whole, and in the compilation of the notes. We are greatly indebted to Dr Simon Keynes, who read a draft of the Introduction and made many helpful corrections and suggestions, and to Mrs Michelle Brown of the Department of Manuscripts at the British Library for her expert advice on both the Cotton and the Harleian manuscripts. We have much appreciated the patience and helpfulness of the General Editors at all stages of the work.

L.W.
M.C.

CONTENTS

ABBREVIATED REFERENCES

ANS	*Proceedings of the Battle Conference on Anglo-Norman Studies*, ed. R. Allen Brown, i–iv (1979–82); continued from 1983 as *Anglo-Norman Studies*
Arch. Jnl.	*The Archaeological Journal*
ASC	*The Anglo-Saxon Chronicle: Two of the Saxon Chronicles Parallel*, ed. C. Plummer and J. Earle (2 vols., Oxford, 1892, 1899); rev. trans., *The Anglo-Saxon Chronicle*, ed. D. Whitelock, D. C. Douglas, S. I. Tucker (London, 1961)
Barlow, *VER*	*The Life of King Edward who rests at Westminster*, ed. Frank Barlow (2nd edn., OMT, 1992)
—— *William Rufus*	Frank Barlow, *William Rufus* (London, 1983)
Bede, *HE*	*Bede's Ecclesiastical History of the English People*, ed. Bertram Colgrave and R. A. B. Mynors (OMT, 1969)
BL	British Library
Blair, 'Secular minster churches'	John Blair, 'Secular minster churches in Domesday Book', *Domesday Book: A Reassessment*, ed. Peter Sawyer (London, 1985), pp. 104–42
Brooks, *Early Church of Canterbury*	Nicholas Brooks, *The Early History of the Church of Canterbury* (Leicester, 1984)
Carmen	*The Carmen de Hastingae Proelio of Guy Bishop of Amiens*, ed. C. Morton and H. Muntz (OMT, 1972)
Cartae Antiquae PRS	*Cartae Antiquae Rolls 11–20*, ed. J. Conway Davies (PRS, new ser. xxxiii, 1960)
CCM	*Corpus Consuetudinum Monasticarum* (Siegburg)
Complete Peerage	*The Complete Peerage of England, Scotland, Ireland, Great Britain and the United Kingdom*, by G. E. C[okayne] (new edn. 13 vols. in 14, 1910–59)
DB	*Domesday Book*, vols. i–ii, ed. A. Farley (London, 1783); vols. iii–iv, ed. H. Ellis (London, 1816)
DHGE	*Dictionnaire d'histoire et de géographie ecclésiastiques*
DLD	*Dialogi Laurentii Dunelmensis monachi et prioris*, ed. J. Raine (Surtees Society, lxx (2), 1878)
DMLBS	*Dictionary of Medieval Latin from British Sources*

Dodwell, *Anglo-Saxon Art*	C. R. Dodwell, *Anglo-Saxon Art: a New Perspective* (Manchester Studies in the History of Art, iii, Manchester, 1982)
Eadmer, *Hist. Nov.*	*Eadmeri historia novorum in Anglia*, ed. M. Rule (RS, 1884)
EEFL	*Enchiridion Eulogicum Fontium Liturgicorum*, ed. Enzo Lodi (Rome, 1979)
EETS	Early English Text Society
EHD	*English Historical Documents*, i, *c.500–1042*, ed. D. Whitelock (2nd edn., London, 1979); ii, *c.1042–1189*, ed. D. C. Douglas and G. W. Greenaway (2nd edn., London, 1981)
EHR	*English Historical Review*
ER	*Essex Review*
Fernie, 'Romanesque church'	E. C. Fernie, 'The romanesque church of Waltham abbey', *JBAA*, cxxxviii (1985), 48–78
Fleming, *Kings and Lords*	Robin Fleming, *Kings and Lords in Conquest England* (Cambridge, 1991)
Florence of Worcester	*Florentii Wigorniensis monachi, Chronicon ex chronicis*, ed. B. Thorpe (English Historical Society, 1848–9)
Freeman, *Norman Conquest*	E. A. Freeman, *The Norman Conquest of England* (2nd edn., 4 vols., Oxford, 1875)
Geary, *Furta Sacra*	Patrick J. Geary, *'Furta Sacra': Thefts of Relics in the Central Middle Ages* (Princeton, NJ, 1978)
Gesta Guillelmi	William of Poitiers, *Gesta Guillelmi ducis Normannorum et regis Anglorum*, ed. Raymonde Foreville (Paris, 1952)
Gesta Stephani	*Gesta Stephani*, ed. K. R. Potter, rev. R. H. C. Davis (OMT, 1976)
Gransden, *Historical Writing*	Antonia Gransden, *Historical Writing in England c.550–1307* (London, 1974)
Hefele–Leclercq	C. J. Hefele, *Histoire des conciles*, ed. H. Leclercq (Paris, 1907–)
IBC	*The Interpreters' Bible Commentary* (4 vols., New York, 1962)
JBAA	*Journal of the British Archaeological Association*
Kemble	J. M. Kemble, *Codex Diplomaticus Aevi Saxonici* (6 vols., English Historical Society Publications, iii, 1839–48)
Keynes, 'Regenbald'	Simon Keynes, 'Regenbald, the chancellor (*sic*)', *ANS* x (1988), 185–222
Knowles, *Monastic Order*	M. D. Knowles, *The Monastic Order in England* (2nd edn., Cambridge, 1963)

LCL | Loeb Classical Library
Lennard, *Rural England* | Reginald Lennard, *Rural England 1066–1135* (Oxford, 1959)
Malmesbury, *Gesta Regum* | *Willelmi Malmesbiriensis de gestis regum Anglorum libri quinque*, ed. W. Stubbs (2 vols., RS, 1887–9)
Mansi | J. D. Mansi, *Sacrorum Conciliorum Nova et Amplissima Collectio* (Venice, 1759–77)
Materials | *Materials for the History of Thomas Becket*, ed. J. C. Robertson and J. B. Sheppard (7 vols., *RS*, 1875–85)
Monasticon | W. Dugdale, *Monasticon Anglicanum*, ed. J. Caley, H. Ellis, and B. Bandinel (6 vols. in 8, London, 1817–30)
NCE | *New Catholic Encyclopedia*
NMT | Nelson's Medieval Texts
OMT | Oxford Medieval Texts
Orbis Latinus | *Orbis Latinus*, ed. H. Plechl (3 vols., Brunswick, 1972)
Orderic | *The Ecclesiastical History of Orderic Vitalis*, ed. M. Chibnall (6 vols., OMT, 1969–80)
PL | *Patrologiae Cursus Completus, Series Latina*, ed. J. P. Migne
PRS | Pipe Roll Society
Ransford, *Waltham Charters* | *The Early Charters of Waltham Abbey 1062–1230*, ed. Rosalind Ransford (Woodbridge, 1989)
Raw, *AS Iconography* | Barbara Raw, *Anglo-Saxon Crucifixion Iconography and the Art of the Monastic Revival* (Cambridge, 1990)
Reg. Chrod. | A. S. Napier, *The Old English Version of the Enlarged Rule of Chrodegang with the Latin Original* (EETS, o.s., cl, Oxford, 1916)
Regesta | *Regesta Regum Anglo-Normannorum*, i, ed. H. W. C. Davis and R. J. Whitwell (Oxford, 1913), iii, ed. H. A. Cronne and R. H. C. Davis (Oxford, 1968)
Robertson, *AS Charters* | *Anglo-Saxon Charters*, ed. A. J. Robertson (2nd edn., Cambridge, 1956)
Rogers, 'Waltham relic-list' | Nicholas Rogers, 'The Waltham abbey relic-list', *England in the Eleventh Century*, ed. Carola Hicks (Harlaxton Medieval Studies, Stamford, 1992), pp. 157–81
RS | Rolls Series
Sawyer | P. H. Sawyer, *Anglo-Saxon Charters: an Annotated*

	List and Bibliography (Royal Historical Society, Guides and Handbooks, viii, London, 1968).
SD	*Symeonis Monachi Opera Omnia*, ed. T. Arnold (2 vols., RS, 1882)
Stubbs	*The Foundation of Waltham Abbey: The Tract 'De Inventione Sanctae Crucis Nostrae'*, ed. W. Stubbs (Oxford and London, 1861)
TEAS	*Transactions of the Essex Archaeological Society*
TRHS	*Transactions of the Royal Historical Society*
VCH	*The Victoria History of the Counties of England*
Vita Haroldi	*Vita Haroldi*, ed. and trans. W. de Gray Birch (London, 1885)
William of Newburgh	William of Newburgh, *Historia rerum Anglicarum*, in *Chronicles of the Reigns of Stephen, Henry II and Richard I*, ed. Richard Howlett (4 vols., RS, 1884–9), vol. i

INTRODUCTION

THE CHURCH OF WALTHAM

AMONG the many foundation histories written by monks and canons in the twelfth century, the Waltham Chronicle, entitled *De inventione sancte crucis*, stands alone, though it has some features in common with the products of monastic houses.[1] It was written by a former canon of the secular college at Waltham after the suppression of the house in 1177 and its replacement by an abbey of Augustinian canons. In part a lament for the extinction of the community in which his life had been spent, it also recounts the history of the 'discovery' at Montacute in the time of King Cnut of the most precious relic of the house, the wonder-working figure of the crucified Christ. So it begins with an account of how the image was brought from Somerset by a great lord, the thegn Tovi the Proud, to his lands at Waltham, and tells of his enrichment of the church that was to become its permanent home.

There is also an underlying political theme in the story, for some time after Tovi's death many of his lands, including Waltham, came into the hands of Harold Godwineson, who founded a college of secular canons in the church. After Harold's defeat at Hastings, his bones were brought, the canons believed, for burial in the church that he had founded.[2] The anonymous writer combined a dirge for a man whom he saw as one endowed with all the qualities of piety, magnanimity, and integrity proper to any benefactor, with a strictly correct attitude towards the Norman dynasty that had supplanted him. It was perhaps fortunate that the presence of the Holy Cross of Waltham, by attracting pilgrims and miracles, could deflect from Harold's tomb any dangerous devotion to a lost cause. The Chronicle could properly include the

---

[1] For references to other foundation histories, see R. W. Southern, 'Aspects of the European tradition of historical writing: 4. The sense of the past', *TRHS* 5th ser., xxiii (1973), 243–64; Gransden, *Historical Writing*, pp. 269–76; for pious legends of origins, see Penelope D. Johnson, 'Pious legends and historical realities: the foundations of La Trinité Vendôme, Bonport and Holyrood', *Revue bénédictine*, xci (1981), 184–93.

[2] See below, pp. xliii–xlvi.

description of miracles, which were an almost indispensable element in works of this kind, without fostering a potentially seditious cult. The translations of Harold's body are reverently recorded, but far from attempting to establish a shrine, the author suggests that one translation may have been deliberately intended to prevent too much devotion being shown at the tomb.[1] Crowland Abbey, which treasured the body of Earl Waltheof after his execution, showed prudent restraint that was very similar.[2]

The legend of the finding of the Holy Cross of Waltham has sometimes been wrongly confused by historians with that of the True Cross. The story of how St Helena, the wife of the Emperor Constantine, discovered the cross of Christ occurs from the fourth century; and the legend of how pieces of the cross were carried all over the Christian world took many forms in the Middle Ages.[3] Waltham may have believed that a fragment of the wood came to the church later, among the relics given by Harold Godwineson.[4] But there is no doubt that the relic discovered at Montacute in the legend handed down by the canons was an *imago Christi*: a figure of the crucified Christ carved in stone. It was evidently life-sized, since we are told that Tovi girded it with his own sword.[5] Other life-sized crucifixes are known to have existed in the Anglo-Saxon period at a number of churches, including Peterborough, Bury, Evesham, and Durham, and miraculous powers were attributed to some.[6] No large figures have survived, and the Waltham crucifix is the earliest of those now lost that can be identified positively in the sources. C. R. Dodwell has suggested Scandinavian influence in its style and ornament.[7] It may have encouraged imitation; Harold's brother Tostig, earl of Northumbria, and his wife Judith gave an *imago crucifixi* to Durham and clothed it with gold and silver.[8] The great cross at Bury St Edmunds, sometimes attributed

---

[1] See below, cap. 21.

[2] Orderic, ii. 347.

[3] The earliest reference to St Helena's 'discovery' is in the funeral oration of St Ambrose for the Emperor Theodosius (*De obitu Theodosii*, 40–8, in *Sancti Ambrosii Episcopi Mediolensis Opera* 18, *Orationes funebres*, ed. O. Faller (Milan and Rome, 1985), pp. 240–7); *NCE* iv. 479–82.

[4] See below, cap. 17.

[5] See below, cap. 12.

[6] On other life-size crucifixes, see Raw, *AS Iconography*, p. 41.

[7] C. R. Dodwell, *Anglo-Saxon Art: a New Perspective* (Manchester Studies in the History of Art, iii, Manchester, 1982), pp. 118–19; G. Schiller, *Iconography of Christian Art*, ii (London, 1972), 140–5.

[8] 'imaginem crucifixi . . . fieri jusserunt, et auro argentoque vestierunt', SD i. 95.

to Abbot Leofstan, is more likely to have been post-Conquest and
to belong to a tradition stemming from Italy. There were close
contacts between the abbey of Bury and Lucca; and the *Vultus
Sanctus* at Lucca (the 'holy face' by which King William Rufus
swore), which was actually a crucifix, would have been seen by
pilgrims passing through on their way to Rome from the time of
Abbot Baldwin.[1] All these, however, were attributed to recent
craftsmen; only the Waltham figure was believed to have been
found.

The central theme in the early chapters of the Waltham chronicle was the history of the wonder-working *imago Christi*. The
author, following the traditions of his community, was not concerned with the history of the original church at Waltham, and
gave a blurred and not always accurate picture of its origins. He
stated that in Tovi's time Waltham itself was little more than a
hunting-lodge, and that the community which grew up around the
newly-built church was cultivating land previously untilled.[2]
Archaeological evidence, however, has shown that the site had
been inhabited for a considerable time; there are traces of a pre-
Christian burial site, and foundations of at least one ground-
standing timber church of the ninth century have been found
below the present church. Possibly a settlement had been dis-
turbed by Viking attacks in the tenth century or even earlier. There
is evidence that a religious house at Nazeing, only three miles from
Waltham, came to an end before the ninth-century invasion.[3] It is
even conceivable that church treasures were carried away from
Waltham and buried at Montacute to save them from the invaders;
this rather than the conventional miracle story that the cart taking
the *imago Christi* from Somerset could not be moved until the name
of Waltham was mentioned, would account for the choice of
Waltham to house the precious relic.[4]

---

[1] Diana M. Webb, 'The Holy Face of Lucca', *ANS* ix (1987), 227–37.

[2] See below, cap. 10. The language of the chronicle is obscure at this point; *pauperis
tugurii* may refer to a very humble place of worship. The word was sometimes used for
the simple huts where hermits or hermit monks lived and prayed in monasteries of the
Columbanian type (cf. Orderic, iii. 270: *Vita Ebrulfi* in Orderic, i. 207).

[3] See P. J. Huggins, 'Excavations of Belgic and Romano-British farm with Middle
Saxon cemetery and churches at Nazeingbury, Essex, 1975–6', *TEAS*, 3rd ser., x (1978),
75; id., with contributions by K. N. Bascombe and R. M. Huggins, 'Excavations of the
collegiate and Augustinian churches, Waltham Abbey, Essex, 1984–87', *Arch. Jnl* cxlvi
(1989), 476–537.

[4] See below, cap. 10.

Tovi the Proud himself was one of Cnut's chief thegns, who witnessed a substantial number of royal charters between 1018 and 1035.[1] A man of wealth and power, he was described as the king's standard-bearer, and acted, on at least one recorded occasion, as the king's messenger.[2] His name normally occurs high in the list of charter witnesses, though usually not quite as high as that of another Scandinavian thegn, Osgod Clapa. There can be no doubt that the Chronicle was correct in describing him as a staller; these were the wealthiest and most prominent men in the king's household, many of whom had administrative duties by virtue of their status. They seem to have been used to integrate regions outside Wessex more fully under royal control.[3] In 1042 he married, almost certainly as his second wife, Gytha, the daughter of Osgod Clapa.[4] Both Osgod and Tovi entered into the confraternity of Thorney Abbey, and their names head the list of a group with Scandinavian names, apparently drawn from Cnut's retinue.[5] Although the Waltham canon exaggerated by describing Tovi as 'secundus a rege' and 'totius Anglie post regem primus', such expressions were used by twelfth-century writers to describe men of considerable power in the royal service,[6] and were probably not taken literally even by their contemporaries. If the implication was that Tovi was a powerful thegn, close to the king and employed on royal business in different parts of the kingdom, this was certainly true. After 1042, when he married Gytha, nothing positive is known of him apart from his benefactions to Waltham. Although a man named Tovi, who was called a staller, witnessed some of the early charters of Edward the Confessor, he was probably a different

[1] Kemble, nos. 728, 730, 743, 744, 753, 749, 1318, 751, 1322; Sawyer, nos. 951, 952, 955, 962, 963, 971, 970, 968, 969, 967, 974, 975.

[2] Robertson, AS Charters, no. 78, pp. 150–3, 400.

[3] For the stallers see Katharin Mack, 'The Stallers: administrative innovation in the reign of Edward the Confessor', Journal of Medieval History, xii (1986), 123–34.

[4] Florence of Worcester, i. 196: '1042. Rex Anglorum Heardecanutus, dum in convivio in quo Osgodus Clapa, magnae vir potentiae, filiam suam Gytham Danico et praepotenti viro Tovio, Prudan cognomento, in loco qui dicitur Lamhythe, magna cum laetitia tradebat nuptui, laetus, sospes et hilaris . . . repente inter bibendum miserabili casu ad terram corruit, et sic mutus permanens sexto idus Junii, feria tertia expiravit . . .'

[5] Dorothy Whitelock, 'Scandinavian personal names in the Liber Vitae of Thorney Abbey', Saga Book of the Viking Society, xii (2) (1937–8), 135–6; Cecily Clark, 'British Library Additional MS. 40,000 ff. iv–12r', ANS vii (1985), 50–68.

[6] Cf. the comments on Ranulf Flambard, listed by R. W. Southern, 'Ranulf Flambard', in Medieval Humanism (Oxford, 1970), pp. 184–5; and those on Geoffrey de Mandeville (Gesta Stephani, pp. 160–2).

man.[1] His name occurs much further down the witness-list than Tovi the Proud's signature had done, and the name was not uncommon. In one charter 'Tovi the White' and 'Tovi the Red' occur simultaneously,[2] and Tovi the sheriff, who was associated with Somerset and may have been a kinsman, occurs later in the reign.[3] The date of Tovi the Proud's marriage feast is fixed by a dramatic event, for during the celebrations King Harthacnut collapsed and died. Tovi may have taken Gytha as a second wife in his old age; and possibly he did not survive for long. His generous benefactions to Waltham may have been motivated partly by the knowledge that his own death was imminent.

The Chronicle contains valuable hints about the sources of Tovi's wealth. In addition to the land he had inherited, the king had given him lands from the royal demesne, and his influence and power had enabled him 'to benefit or harm anyone he wished'.[4] Evidently he was able, on a much smaller scale, to enrich himself by the same methods as Earl Godwine and his sons, who 'were able to appropriate sizeable chunks of territory with the aid or consent of their aristocratic allies' and who 'also pursued both less legal and more royally controlled forms of acquisition'.[5] Some property they seized, some was granted by the king, and some came from the estates set aside for royal officials—in Tovi's case, for stallers. The stallership may have been hereditary; Tovi's grandson Asgar was called 'the staller' in charters from 1044.[6] Tovi's son Athelstan may also have been a staller, as the chronicler believed, although it is unlikely that he can be identified as 'Ælfstan the staller', who witnessed some charters in the early years of King Edward's reign. All that the Chronicle tells us of Athelstan is that he inherited only the property belonging to the stallership, and lost many possessions through his insufficiency. It would be interesting to know whether, if Tovi died before 1046, his

---

[1] Kemble, no. 1332 (1042), where 'Tovi minister' first occurs far down the list after Ordgar, Ælfgar, Godwine, Æthelric, and Toky, nos. 792 (1050), 791 (1050), 800 (1054).

[2] Robertson, AS Charters, p. 400; Kemble, no. 741, is signed by 'Tovi hwita' and 'Tovi reada'.

[3] F. E. Harmer, Anglo-Saxon Writs (Manchester, 1952), pp. 134, 281–5; DB, i. 87b, 88, 91, 94, 98, 99; Kemble, nos. 821, 837, 839.

[4] See below, cap. 14.

[5] Fleming, Kings and Lords, pp. 83–4.

[6] Kemble, no. 872; Stubbs, p. 13 n. 42. He attests charters of King Edward, sometimes as minister, once as regiae procurator aulae (Kemble, no. 813), and once as regis dapifer (Kemble, no. 808). His name is variously spelled, as Ansgar, Esger, Esegar.

son and heir Athelstan was involved in rebellion with Osgod Clapa that year and shared Osgod's subsequent exile, or at least forfeited his estates.[1] Many, including Waltham and Hitchin, were given to Harold Godwineson. Whatever may have happened, however, Asgar was in favour before the Norman Conquest, and in 1066 held many of Tovi's old estates, particularly those in Essex.[2] If Tovi held some lands in Somerset, as the chronicler claimed, no certain evidence of them has survived, unless Tovi the sheriff was a kinsman.

Clearer written evidence of the church at Waltham begins only with Tovi's work to rehouse the *imago Christi*. The process of foundation or refoundation is compressed in the Chronicle. Tovi's enterprise began in the reign of Cnut, before 1035; but the events described when Tovi and Gytha showered wealth upon the church must have taken place after their wedding in 1042.[3] The eleventh century was a time of vigorous church building, and the simple categories of churches as classified in the earlier laws soon became blurred.[4] King Edgar had distinguished three types only: the 'old minster, to which obedience is due', a thegn's church with a graveyard, and a church without a graveyard. Æthelred II, in 1014, elaborated further; his laws recognized the head minster, the minster of medium rank, the lesser church with a graveyard, and the field chapel. But 'the contrast between the ancient minsters and the manorial churches was losing its significance for the organization of pastoral functions'.[5] Tovi's church at Waltham would probably have been classified as a lesser minster of the type to which St Michael's and St Peter's churches at Shrewsbury appear to have belonged.[6] It acted as a parish church for the

[1] For Osgod's rebellion, exile, and death, see Florence of Worcester, i. 200, 202. Stubbs suggested very tentatively that Ælfstan, who was *stallere* about 1044 (Kemble, no. 773), might just possibly have been Athelstan (Stubbs, p. 13 n. 42). Although it is unlikely that anyone writing in the 11th cent. would have written Athelstan for Ælfstan, it is just conceivable that the distortion could have occurred in the 12th cent.

[2] He also held estates in seven other counties; after the Conquest most were given to Geoffrey (I) de Mandeville (*VCH Essex*, i. 343; Robertson, *AS Charters*, p. 464).

[3] See below, caps. 12, 13.

[4] On the pre-Conquest minsters and other churches, see John Blair, 'Secular minster churches in Domesday Book', *Domesday Book: A Reassessment*, ed. Peter Sawyer (London, 1985), pp. 104–42; Reginald Lennard, *Rural England 1066–1135* (Oxford, 1959), pp. 300–1; John Blair, 'From minster to parish church', *Minsters and Parish Churches: The Local Church in Transition*, ed. John Blair (Oxford, 1988), pp. 1–19; Emma Mason, *Saint Wulfstan of Worcester* (Oxford, 1990), p. 9.

[5] Lennard, *Rural England*, p. 300.

[6] Steve Basset, 'Anglo-Saxon Shrewsbury and its churches', *Midland History*, xvi (1991), 1–23, at pp. 13–14.

inhabitants of the township that grew up around it,[1] but it was itself served by a small group of clergy enjoying a very close relationship with the lord of the land. Like such churches as Moreville and Taunton, its exact status is not entirely clear.[2] Tovi appointed two priests with assistant clerks to serve God in the church; and he and his wife devoted themselves to its enrichment. What exactly is implied by the statement in the Chronicle that he was joined by his devotion in the fellowship of the clergy is not clear. Then and later many lay men and women were included in the 'fraternity' of monasteries and associated in the prayers of monks, as Tovi, Osgod Clapa, and many more were with Thorney. Some similar association may have linked benefactors with groups of secular clergy.[3] On the position at Waltham the records are silent. There is no mention in the Chronicle of Tovi's burial, or of any tomb at Waltham, which in view of his benefactions is surprising, unless indeed he died in exile.

A new phase in the history of the church began after Harold Godwineson refounded the house as a college of secular canons. The movement to organize clerks into communities living a regular life had begun on the continent in the eighth century, when Chrodegang, bishop of Metz (d. 766), caused the canons of his cathedral to live a common life, and drew up a rule for their guidance.[4] After the promulgation of the rule in the council of Aix-la-Chapelle of 816, it was adapted and modified for much wider use among colleges of clergy not attached to a cathedral. England, however, lay outside the regions touched by the decisions of the council; and the rule as practised there seems at first to have been nearer to the shorter original rule of Chrodegang. At first this was little used in England, except possibly at Canterbury.[5] However, a copy of the englarged *Regula* was known at Winchester before the

---

[1] See below, cap. 28 and p. 75 n. 3.

[2] Lennard, *Rural England*, p. 301.

[3] See above, p. xvi n. 5. For some early English gilds attached to town churches, see *EHD* i. 603–7.

[4] *Sancti Chrodegangi Metensis Episcopi Regula Canonicorum*, ed. L. d'Achéry (*PL* lxxxix, 1097–1120). For an Old English translation with Latin text, see *Reg. Chrod.* For the history of the Rule, see Albert Werminghoff, 'Die Beschlüsse des Aachener Concils im Jahre 816', *Neues Archiv der Gesellschaft für ältere deutsche Geschichtskunde*, xxvii (1902), 607–75; Gaston Hocquard, 'Le règle de Saint Chrodegang: État de quelques questions', in *Saint Chrodegang: Communications présentées au Colloque tenu à Metz à l'occasion du douzième centenaire de sa mort* (Metz, 1967), pp. 55–89; Ch. Dereine, 'Chanoines', *DHGE* xii (1953), 364–75.

[5] Brooks, *Early Church of Canterbury*, pp. 51–2, 155–6.

end of the tenth century, and was used by reformers such as Bishop Æthelwold to regulate secular clergy.[1] It was soon translated into English, and its use spread in England during the eleventh century, especially after the Council of Rome of 1059 repeated Leo IX's demand for clerical chastity and exhorted the clergy to hold their revenues in common and adopt a regular life, with common refectory and dormitory near to their church.[2]

The enlarged *Regula* was also widely used in Lotharingia, and Earl Harold may have known of it from his contacts with the Lotharingian churches, whose strict discipline he greatly admired. When he decided to found a college of secular canons he was at the height of his power and influence. Indeed, the wealth of the Godwine family was greater than that of the king. Harold held the earldom of East Anglia until his father's death, when he became earl of Wessex. His extensive holdings in Essex in 1066 suggest that he retained many of the properties he had acquired there even after surrendering the earldom of East Anglia.[3] An earl's duties included defence, and Harold held many strong points along the south coast as well as the East Anglian estates that were intended to provide for the defence of shores and inlets vulnerable to Danish attack. Waltham, in the Lea Valley, was one of these. The wish to found a religious house was natural in any great magnate; quite apart from any feelings of piety, such a foundation would enhance his prestige and status. Harold might have chosen to imitate the king, who was actively rebuilding Westminster Abbey as his memorial and intended burial place; but houses of secular canons could serve a great lord in practical ways by training clerks for his private chapel and writing office.[4] And whereas Westminster owed much to Edward's contacts with Normandy, where he had lived in exile and seen something of the great Benedictine revival, Harold's travels had taken him to other parts of Europe.

---

[1] The principal surviving MS of the *Regula*, Corpus Christi College Cambridge 191, which was written for Leofric, bishop of Exeter, was copied from a 10th-cent. exemplar compiled at the Old Minster, Winchester, as the list of names illustrating church officers in ch. 2 (including *Wulfstan cantor*) makes clear. We are grateful to Michael Lapidge for this information.

[2] Mansi, xix. 879; Hefele–Leclerq, iv (2), 1186–9, canons 3, 4.

[3] Fleming, *Kings and Lords*, pp. 56–7.

[4] For the numerous houses of secular clerks founded in Normandy at this time, see L. Musset, 'Recherches sur les communautés de clercs seculiers en Normandie au xie siècle', *Bulletin de la Société des Antiquaires de Normandie*, lv (1961), 5–38; Blair, 'Secular minster churches', pp. 123–4.

He was possibly in Flanders in 1056, when he may have appeared at the court of Count Baldwin V and have gone on to accompany Baldwin into Germany.[1] Later he went on a pilgrimage to Rome.[2] His possibly involuntary visit to Normandy depicted in the Bayeux Tapestry was made after the foundation of Waltham, so he is unlikely to have had firsthand knowledge of the upsurge of monastic foundations there, whereas he had certainly seen something of the houses of canons in Lotharingia.

His reasons for choosing Waltham are not immediately obvious. The principal manor of Earl Godwine's family was in Wessex, at Bosham, with good moorings by Thorney island where the family's ships could come to port. From this manor Harold sailed when he embarked on the expedition that led to his capture by Guy of Ponthieu and rescue by Duke William of Normandy.[3] There was a religious community (first heard of in the time of Bede) at Bosham. Though apparently much decayed by the eleventh century, the value of its property was assessed for sixty-five hides.[4] The church had, however, been given by King Edward to his Norman chaplain Osbern, and though it was to be restored as a college for six secular canons in the reign of Henry I it was perhaps never in Harold's direct control.[5] Tovi's church had come to Harold after Tovi's son Athelstan lost most of his inheritance, and it may already have been becoming a centre of pilgrimage because of its possession of the Holy Cross. Whatever the reasons, Harold chose it as the place for his reformed house of secular canons, provided a lavish endowment out of the wealth that he had acquired, sometimes by dubious means, and recruited some of the first canons from Lotharingia.

According to the Chronicle Earl Harold added eleven clerks to the two appointed by Tovi, so that the community consisted of a dean and twelve canons.[6] They included Master Adelard, a German who had studied at Utrecht, and he was asked to establish

---

[1] P. Grierson, 'A visit of Earl Harold to Flanders in 1056', *EHR* li (1936), 90–7. His conclusions have been questioned by Sten Körner, *The Battle of Hastings, England and Europe* (Lund, 1964), pp. 205–6.

[2] Although the truth of the story of Harold's pilgrimage to Rome has been questioned, the *Vita Ædwardi regis* states positively that 'Romam ad confessionem apostolorum processit'. Otherwise it is mentioned only in the unreliable *Vita Haroldi*, cap. 7, where it is obviously confused with Tostig's visit (Barlow, *VER*, cap. 5, p. 33 and n. 5).

[3] *The Bayeux Tapestry*, ed. David Wilson (London, 1985), pls. 2, 3.

[4] *DB* i. 17b; *VCH Sussex*, i. 392.

[5] *VCH Sussex*, ii. 109–10.

[6] See below, caps. 14, 15.

at Waltham the 'rules, ordinances and customs' of the Lotharingian church. The details given in various chapters of the Chronicle show that the influence of the *Regula canonicorum* of Chrodegang in the new college persisted well into the twelfth century, when the anonymous chronicler himself entered the community. A substantial part of the endowment provided by Earl Harold came from Tovi's former lands. In 1060 the gifts were confirmed and augmented by King Edward, and a charter of endowment was issued in 1062.[1] The estates and their boundaries are listed in the royal diploma, which has survived only in later cartulary copies. Earl Harold added rich gifts of church ornaments, vestments, and relics. Anglo-Saxon craftsmen were famous for their skills, and their goldsmiths were pre-eminent. Both the description in later chronicles and the few surviving examples of pre-Conquest metalwork show that the chronicler exaggerated very little if at all in his wonder at the earl's gifts.[2] These included, besides many chalices, candlesticks, censers, and crosses all made of gold or silver, and many richly embroidered vestments, twelve statues of Apostles cast to support the front of a magnificent altar made of pure gold, and lions similarly cast to support the rear.[3]

The endowments were intended to support a dean and twelve canons, whose customs as recorded in the Chronicle seem to have been derived from the enlarged *Regula*. There are, however, no precise citations, and the prescriptions of the *Regula* had become modified either before they were first applied or before the Waltham chronicler joined the community. It is not clear from his language whether he used any written record at this point, or was simply recording the way of life he had known from the second quarter of the twelfth century. Whatever the truth of this, the imprint of the *Regula* remained in the customs he described. The *Regula* insisted on a common life, with the canons dining together and sharing a dormitory, though the bishop could, if it seemed reasonable to him, allow them to sleep in *dispositas mansiones*, which

[1] See below, pp. xxxviii–xliii.

[2] See Dodwell, *Anglo-Saxon Art*, pp. 118–19, 180–9, 202–5; Eadmer (*Hist. Nov.*, pp. 109–10) describes the magnificent cope which had been given to the bishop of Benevento in the reign of Cnut, 'cappam . . . valde pretiosam, aurifrigio ex omni parte ornatam'.

[3] See below, cap. 16. For the decoration of churches with life-size figures, see Raw, *AS Iconography*, pp. 16–17.

appear to have been houses within the church precincts.[1] The leaders of the community, who represented the bishop, were expected to set a good example of a holy way of life in faith, love, and chastity. The *Regula* names the *primicerius* (later replaced by the *praepositus*) and the archdeacon.[2] They needed to be sufficiently learned in the Gospels and the canonical precepts of the Fathers to instruct their community in the *lex divina* and *lectio divina*. Several clauses insisted on the orderly conduct of all services in the church, the reverent singing of the psalms, and the discipline of the boys who were being educated in the community.[3] For those who transgressed in any way a disciplinary code was laid down, with punishments ranging from admonition through corporal chastisement to severe penance and excommunication.[4] The food allowances included meat except at times of fast, and were sufficient to allow the canons to support needy people.[5] There was, however, no suggestion of families being tolerated; while the *Regula* allowed canons for good reason and with permission to spend some time in separate houses within the precincts, women were not admitted to the enclosure at any time.[6] If these rules were applied when Waltham was first founded, they had certainly been stretched by the early twelfth century. The food allowances have justly been described as gargantuan, and would certainly have supported families as well as some paupers.[7] Cash allowances had replaced the annual issue of clothes and shoes in the *Regula*.[8] Marriage had become widespread; indeed Master Adelard himself had a son Peter.[9] The repeated insistence of the chronicler himself, however, on the virtue of chastity shows that some at least of the community were opposed to marriage.

The endowments given for the church are described in the foundation charter of 1062. Tovi's provision for his church, with its two priests and assistant clerks, had been modest. According to the chronicler, he gave some land in Waltham, with Loughton, Alderton, Hitchin, and Lambeth, and a place called *Chenlevedene*, which is usually identified as Kelvedon.[10] Since there is no hint in any other source that the canons ever held any land in either of the two

---

[1] *Reg. Chrod.*, cap. 11.   [2] Caps. 8, 44.
[3] Caps. 2, 12, 22, 23, 24.   [4] Caps. 26, 27, 31, 50.
[5] Cap. 6.   [6] Cap. 11.
[7] Knowles, *Monastic Order*, p. 463.
[8] See below, cap. 25 and *Reg. Chrod.*, cap. 39.
[9] See below, cap. 25.   [10] See below, cap. 12.

Essex Kelvedons, which were Westminster manors, it seems at least possible that the name was a local name attached to some new settlement in the forest in the vicinity of Waltham. The church received a small, fairly compact central group of estates carved out of the forest, at Waltham, Loughton, and Alderton; and perhaps *Chenlevedene* was in the neighbourhood of the place known as Typpedene or Debden, which is now part of the parish of Loughton.[1] There were also outliers at Lambeth, where Tovi's marriage had been celebrated, and Hitchin; both these manors were among those lost by Tovi's son. Some were given to Harold, who made ample provision out of his augmented estates for his house of twelve canons; and King Edward was said to have restored Lambeth and Hitchin.

The manors were organized to provide regular food farms for the canons, and some were assigned to particular prebends. The estates of the dean at South Weald, Paslow, and Arlesey were made responsible for the farm of nineteen weeks; he also received West Waltham because of his obligation to provide hospitality.[2] Of the canons' prebends, Netteswell was to provide for seven weeks and two days, Alderton for four weeks and two days, Upminster for two weeks and two days, Woodford for two weeks, Loughton for one week and one day, Debden for two weeks, and Brickenden for two weeks: a total of forty weeks. This still left twelve weeks unaccounted for; possibly they were covered by the provisions from 'Northland' in Waltham, where each canon had fifteen acres. The farm system described in the chronicle as dating from the time of the foundation may have developed later;[3] if it belongs to the time

---

[1] Stubbs, p. 11 n. 32. Both Kelvedon and Kelvedon Hatch were Westminster manors; Kelvedon had been given by Guthmund before 1066 and Kelvedon Hatch was the gift of Ailric, chamberlain, *c.* 1066 (Barbara Harvey, *Westminster Abbey and its Estates in the Middle Ages* (Oxford, 1977), pp. 342–3). There is no sign that either had anything to do with Tovi. While the name *Cynlaevedene* or *Cynlavedyne* occurs, as far as is known, only for Kelvedon, elements of the name occur elsewhere in the district (*Cherleslega*, *Chelveston*, *Cealvadune* (see P. Reaney, *Place Names of Essex* (Cambridge, 1935), pp. 58, 573, 575); and in a region of clearings in the woods where meadows and swine denes were common the scribe may have discovered the name in a list of boundaries, or incorrectly transcribed it.

[2] The returns in the Domesday Survey record that in 1066 West Waltham had been held by 'Unwin, a canon' from Earl Harold; and it is possible that the reference is meant to be Wulwin, the dean of Waltham mentioned in the Chronicle. The fact that the Chronicle lists West Waltham alone after describing the farm system may imply that it was held by the dean in a different way from the remainder of the endowments; and there is no suggestion in Domesday Book that the other Waltham manors of Paslow Hall, South Weald, and Arlesey were held by the dean directly from Harold.

[3] See below, cap. 15.

when many or all of the canons had separate houses it may imply
that all were obliged to reside for three months each year, when
they could have been supported by the food farms from 'Northland'.[1] It is not entirely clear from references to the clergy hurrying
to the church when the bell for Mattins was rung whether they all
came from nearby houses. The description of the boys arriving in
procession from their school in the same way as canons rising in
the night might possibly imply a procession of some canons at least
from the dormitory.[2] So while some of the precepts of Chrodegang's *Regula* relating to the studies of the canons, the orderly
conduct of church offices, and the punishments for trivial or more
serious offences survived, it is clear from the Chronicle that the
secular canons had allowed some latitude to creep into their way of
life in the century after the foundation of the college. And we
cannot be sure that Chrodegang's *Regula* had not been only loosely
applied from the first, as at Christchurch (Hants) and many
Norman colleges.[3]

Harold's death in battle at Hastings only a few years after the
foundation left the canons without a protector. The chronicler's
ignorance of the events leading up to the battle is apparent from
his belief that Tostig, whom Harold defeated and killed at Stamford Bridge, was fighting at Harold's side against the Normans.
The community, however, had cherished its legends, and the
canons firmly believed that the image of Christ had bowed its head
in sorrow when Harold prayed in the church before meeting Duke
William's forces in battle.[4] They also believed, probably with good
reason, that Harold's body had been brought back from the battlefield and buried in the church at Waltham. In the difficult years
after the English defeat some of the estates of the canons were lost.
King William gave some, including lands in Waltham and Millo
to Walcher, bishop of Durham, to provide him with a base near
London, and they passed to Walcher's successor in the see,
William of Saint-Calais.[5] William Rufus despoiled the church of

---

[1] Houses outside the close in the region of Northland are mentioned in the charter of
Henry II for the reformed church of Augustinian canons (1077), 'Apud Waltham terram
que dicitur Norland, mansiones que fuerunt canonicorum secularium' (*Cartae Antiquae*
PRS, no. 357).

[2] See below, caps. 28, 25.

[3] John Blair, 'Secular minster churches', p. 134.

[4] See below, cap. 20.

[5] Ransford, *Waltham Charters*, pp. xxiv, xxxv.

some of its treasures and gave them to the royal abbey of Saint-Étienne-de-Caen.[1] If the rebuilding of the church began in the late eleventh century, he may have made some restoration; but if the building dated from the first decade of the twelfth century, a full recovery was delayed until the reign of Henry I.[2] Henry assigned Waltham to the queen's dower, and both he and his pious queen, Matilda, increased its privileges and endowments.[3] The links with Durham were not sharply broken; the names of a number of canons occur as late additions in the Durham *Liber Vitae*, and the architecture of the new church shows a strong resemblance to that of Durham's rebuilt cathedral. Laurence of Durham, who was educated at Waltham and was for a time a canon there, finally chose to become a monk at Durham.[4]

The new church was designed to provide a setting for the Holy Cross as well as serving the needs of the canons. The apse had a simple ambulatory without radiating chapels, which left room for processions; it was of a type rare in England, though there was a similar apse at Lichfield cathedral. This may imply that the canons already spent much time in prebendal churches and celebrated mass there. Three new 'bubble chapels' were added in the early twelfth century, to provide an eastern chapel for the Holy

---

[1] See below, cap. 22.

[2] For the discussion of the dates of rebuilding, see P. J. Huggins, K. N. Bascombe, and R. M. Huggins, 'Excavations of the collegiate and Augustinian churches, Waltham Abbey, Essex', *Arch. Jnl*, cxlvi, 476–537, who suggest that building may have begun in the early 1090s, since the tithes from the inhabitants of Waltham, where heads of families numbered 126 in 1086, could have paid for sufficient masons, carpenters, and labourers to undertake building work.

[3] Ransford, *Waltham Charters*, nos. 3, 4, 5, 6, 7, 8, 10, 15.

[4] He was remembered as a poet and musician, as well as a successful administrator and prior of Durham; see *DLD*, pp. xxvii–xxxvi. His description of Waltham is printed below, Appendix I. The end pages bound into BL Harley MS 491 are *membra disiecta* of a Durham mortuary roll. One fragment (fo. 47ᵛ) reads, 'Titulus sancte crucis ecclesie Walthamensis. Anima eius et anime fidelium defunctorum requiescant in pace. Orate pro fratribus nostris Waltero decano, Adalardo magistro, Osgoto et [. . .].

Non versus inopes rerum nugeque canore
Proficient anime sed pia nomina sua.'

The name of Harold is added between the lines over 'Walter'. Walter the dean occurs 1100 × 1108, and was certainly dead before 1115 (Ransford, *Waltham Charters*, p. x). Adelard was master in the early schools (above, p. xxi). Osgot may be Osgod Cnoppe, who was sent to bring Harold's body back to Waltham (below, cap. 20). The other legible entries in the fragment, which are all of continental houses, are, Notre-Dame Laon; St Vincent Laon; St Laumer Blois: St Florent (? Saumur); St Quentin (? Vermandois). For a description of Harley 491 see R. A. B. Mynors, *Durham Cathedral Manuscripts to the End of the Twelfth Century* (Oxford, 1939), p. 60, no. 84.

Cross and two other altars in the side chapels. This extension of the east end probably took place in the 1120s, when Harold's tomb was moved for the second time, apparently to avoid attracting the attention of pilgrims coming to the Holy Cross. The rebuilding of the nave, from east to west, continued in the early twelfth century; it provided a parish church for the inhabitants of the little town of Waltham.[1] This second nave may have been the inspiration for the description given in the Chronicle of Tovi's church, which the author had never known. His account of how Harold ornamented the capitals of the columns and the bases and 'twists' of the arches 'using bronze plate and gold inlaid everywhere' might have been applied to the post-Conquest Romanesque church with its chevron decoration, but not to the plainer Saxon arches which must have existed in the earlier building. On the other hand, as Stubbs suggested, this part of the description may have referred to a ciborium among the treasures of the canons, though the chronicler, possibly using a written record at this point, thought it applied to the church itself.[2]

Waltham did not escape the disturbances of Stephen's reign. Stephen gave it to his queen, Matilda;[3] and the empress in her brief period of power attempted to restore it to her step-mother, the dowager queen Adeliza, who had taken William d'Aubigny *pincerna* as her second husband.[4] D'Aubigny, a steady supporter of Stephen in spite of his wife's loyalties, came into conflict with his most powerful neighbour, Geoffrey de Mandeville II, earl of Essex.[5] When Earl Geoffrey finally turned against Stephen in the autumn of 1143 his rivalry with d'Aubigny brought war and ravaging into the district. The local inhabitants carried their possessions into the church for safety when Flemish mercenaries overran the little town and Earl Geoffrey set fire to the houses.[6] In spite of living through these scenes, the Waltham chronicler wrote with admiration of Earl Geoffrey's character: a tribute which is all the

---

[1] See Huggins and Bascombe, p. 510; Fernie, 'Romanesque church', pp. 48–78; *VCH Essex*, v. 171–2.

[2] See below, cap. 16; Fernie, 'Romanesque church', p. 54; Stubbs, n. 67.

[3] *Regesta*, iii, no. 915.   [4] *Regesta*, iii, no. 918.

[5] William I gave some of the estates of Asgar the staller to Geoffrey (I) de Mandeville; and although he forfeited them later, by 1141 his son had succeeded in recovering them (C. Warren Hollister, 'The misfortunes of the Mandevilles', *Monarchy, Magnates and Institutions in the Anglo-Norman World* (London and Ronceverte, 1986), pp. 117–27, repr. from *History*, lviii (1973), 18–28).

[6] See below, cap. 30.

more remarkable since the only other contemporary who did not denounce the earl as a brutal and lawless ravager was the chronicler of his own foundation at Walden where he was respected as a patron.[1] This was a difficult period for the canons; and even Henry of Blois, bishop of Winchester, who for a time added the deanery of Waltham to his other church benefices, did nothing to preserve or enrich it. Indeed, the chronicler's only mention of him was to state that he had tried unsuccessfully to purchase a precious jewel from the Holy Cross and carry it off to Winchester.[2]

The Chronicle ends in 1144, and the next thirty years have left almost no record of life in the college. After the murder of Archbishop Thomas Becket, Henry II vowed to make reparation by founding religious houses. He obtained papal permission to replace the house of secular canons at Waltham with an abbey of Augustinian canons.[3] The charges of loose living brought against the dean and canons at that time may have meant no more than that many were married; and in the changed moral climate of the later twelfth century clerical marriage had become unacceptable.[4] The chronicler's repeated insistence on the virtue of celibacy may have been due to his belief that loss of virginity had caused the canons to forfeit their lifelong home. One protest that they had faithfully guarded the treasures of the church even though they had been demoted for their sins may imply that a further charge of dissipating the wealth of the church was made by their critics.[5]

The end for the secular canons came in 1177. On 20 January, after King Henry had obtained a bull from Pope Alexander III authorizing the refoundation, Dean Geoffrey Rufus resigned the

---

[1] *Monasticon*, iv. 141–2. An edition of *The Book of the Foundation of Walden Abbey* is being prepared for OMT by Leslie Watkiss and Diana Greenway.

[2] See below, cap. 13. By papal permission Henry of Blois held the abbey of Glastonbury as well as the bishopric of Winchester, and he also added to them the deanery of St Martin le Grand in London.

[3] At Avranches, when he became reconciled to the pope, Henry II vowed to go on a crusade. According to Gerald of Wales (*Opera*, viii, ed. G. F. Warner (RS, 1891), p. 170), he received permission to commute this vow by founding three monasteries. Gerald alleged that he fulfilled it cheaply by refounding the houses of secular canons at Waltham and Amesbury, and adding a new Carthusian house at Witham. The version of Roger of Howden (*Gesta Henrici Secundi Benedicti abbatis*, ed. W. Stubbs (RS, 1867), i. 134–5) is different: Henry had vowed to found a house of regular canons for the remission of his sins.

[4] On the marriage of secular canons in the 11th and 12th cents. see, most recently, Christopher N. L. Brooke, *The Medieval Idea of Marriage* (Oxford, 1989), pp. 78–89, and works there cited.

[5] See below, cap. 13.

deanery of Waltham into the king's hand, and Henry made provision for him and the canons. They were allowed either to keep their prebends for life, or to receive compensation in exchange for them. On 11 June sixteen Augustinian canons drawn from Cirencester, Osney, and St Osyth, were introduced into the church to replace them, and a great building work began to provide for a larger community in due course.[1]

Incidental references make it plain that the Chronicle was written partly at least to ensure that the past glories of the house should not be forgotten by the new occupants, and that they should appreciate their inheritance. Whether the chronicler remained in his old prebend or accepted a pension, he regarded it as a privilege even more than a duty to record the traditions he had treasured from boyhood and the miracles performed in the church. The survival of his book, even in what may be a truncated form, is fortunate, not least because within a generation far less reliable traditions had been collected and embodied in the *Vita Haroldi*. Even though some of the early legends in the Chronicle are historically unreliable, the work is important both as a foundation history and for the information it contains about the secular college and its patrons, the way of life of the canons, and the organization of their estates.

THE AUTHOR OF THE CHRONICLE

The author of the Chronicle entered Waltham in 1124 as a boy of five, through the gift of Queen Adeliza.[2] His entry guaranteed him a prebend in due course. It appears to have been normal for the boys in the school to become canons of Waltham if they so wished;[3] some at least, like Master Adelard's son Master Peter, were the sons of canons. When the *Regula canonicorum* was adopted in many secular Frankish churches after 816, the schools for boys provided one means of educating future clergy. The college at Waltham appears to have had a well-stocked library, if

---

[1] Ransford, *Waltham Charters*, pp. xxiv–xxv, nos. 26, 51; *Papsturkunden in England*, ed. W. Holtzmann, i (Berlin, 1930), no. 174; *VCH Essex*, ii. 167.

[2] See below, caps. 11, 20, 25. He said, when the college was dissolved in 1177, that he had entered it fifty-three years earlier as a boy of five.

[3] The chronicler stated (below, cap. 25) that the prebends were in the queen's gift, and that he had received one.

the catalogue made at the beginning of the thirteenth century contained many books that went back to the early days of the house.[1] In common with the great Benedictine libraries, it contained a good selection of the works of the early Fathers together with the Bible and biblical commentaries; but in addition it was better provided with the writings of classical Latin authors and with works used in the study of grammar and rhetoric. A commentary on Quintilian, *De causis*,[2] attributed to 'Adelard' may have been the work of Master Adelard himself, and he may also have contributed two or three books on medicine. A selection of over twenty volumes, headed *De auctoribus*, included works by Horace, Juvenal, Persius, and Sallust, the *Ilias Latina*[3] as well as the more common *Aeneid* of Vergil, and an exceptionally large number of works by Ovid. This may account for the Vergilian and Prudentian reminiscences, and for the tendency of the chronicler to use constructions that he could have found in the poets, though his style on the whole is a characteristic product of twelfth-century teaching, and in the more rhetorical passages slips into rhyming prose.[4] His occasional poems show him to have been a competent versifier; his poem on the death of Harold shows an Ovidian adeptness in the rhetorical use of words.[5]

Although discipline had declined for a time, probably in the period of disruption after the Norman conquest, it had been restored by the time the chronicler entered the community. His incidental references to his own life and experience show that some at least of the customs prescribed by Chrodegang's *Regula* survived, even though celibacy was no longer strictly observed and

[1] Printed by M. R. James, 'Manuscripts from Essex monastic libraries', *TEAS*, new ser., xxi (1937), 40–5.

[2] Quintilian in his *Institutio oratoria*, vi, Preface, 3, referred to *librum, quem de causis corruptae eloquentiae emisi* (see also *Inst. orat.* xii. 23). This book has not survived; the *Dialogus de oratoribus* of Tacitus was frequently thought by medieval writers to be the *De causis*, and was wrongly attributed to Quintilian (see P. Cornelii Taciti, *Dialogus de oratoribus*, ed. Alain Michel (Paris, 1962), pp. 1–2). The reference in the Waltham catalogue is probably to the *Dialogus de oratoribus* of Tacitus.

[3] See *Texts and Transmission: a Survey of the Latin Classics*, ed. L. D. Reynolds (Oxford, 1983), pp. 191–4. A copy of this work was noted in the Durham library catalogue (ibid., p. 192); the Waltham volume may have been copied from it.

[4] Cf. Tovi's prayer before the Holy Cross (below, cap. 12): 'Adoro te, Domine, infernum *uisitantem* et in sanctis animabus inferos *triumphantem*; Adoro te a mortuis *resurgentem*, morte tua mortem fidelium *consummantem*; Adoro te in celum *ascendentem* ad consessum patris et abinde spiritum tuum in corda discipulorum et eorum pure sequatium *mittentem*.'

[5] See below, cap. 20.

the canons had their own houses. The boys in the school were firmly disciplined: they were required to 'walk, stand, read and sing in a becoming and dignified manner'. Whilst in the choir they were not permitted to look at each other, let alone talk, and the procession to and from the schools and the choir had to be orderly 'like canons rising in the night'.[1] Both he and his contemporary, Laurence of Durham, remembered their early years at Waltham as a happy time. Although Laurence went on to the stricter life of a monk at Durham, he wrote of Waltham as a place he had loved. The church, he says, was surrounded by well-ordered orchards and gardens: there were pear trees, vines, fig trees and chestnut trees, oaks, mulberries, and nut bushes, as well as beautifully laid out vegetable gardens. He praises the grandeur of the church's architecture, remarking that even Daedalus himself would have been amazed to see it, and describes the beauty of the interior, decorated with gold, silver, and bronze, and hung with tapestries.[2]

The author of the chronicle, like the other boys, first carried out the duties of an acolyte and took his turn as censer.[3] He had become a canon with a house of his own by the time he was about twenty-five.[4] Whether or not he married is not clear: his repeated praise of the virtue of celibacy is balanced by general laments for sins that have led to the community being replaced by religious of a stricter order. His chronicle throws a little light incidentally on the routine life of the canons. References to some of the night offices and to Mattins, Vespers, and possibly Compline[5] suggest that the canons preserved much of the regular liturgy prescribed in Chrodegang's *Regula*, which was in places closely modelled on that of the Benedictine houses. A few officers are named, including two deans, Wulwin and Henry of Blois, and the masters in the schools, Adelard and his son Peter.[6] The choirmaster is mentioned and three sacristans are named. Turkill, the old sacristan who must have been eighty or ninety when he died *c.* 1125, recounted to the boys his memories of the events of 1066 when the figure on the

[1] See below, cap. 25.
[2] See below, Appendix I.
[3] See below, cap. 28.
[4] He mentioned that his own house was damaged by the fire during the disturbances of 1143–4; see below, cap. 30.
[5] The reference (below, cap. 27) to the singing of Compline may refer to the office in the nunnery of Wix.
[6] Æthelric Childemaister, one of the two canons sent to ask William the Conqueror for Harold's body (below, cap. 20), seems from his name to have had charge of the boys.

cross was said to bow its head, and described Harold's gifts to the church.[1] A few years later the sacristan Anthony, also called *custos ecclesie* in the same passage, detected the theft from the altar by Edith Crickel and recovered the stolen coin.[2] Apparently the sacristan had duties like those of the monastic sacristans, who were responsible for the candles and some of the oblations in the church.[3] Anthony, as *custos*, also had the duty of unlocking and opening the church doors. By 1143 another sacristan, called Warmund, appears.[4] There was also a *custos dormitorii* who, like those at Cluny, was probably required to make sure that clothing kept in the dormitory was not lost or stolen.[5] By 1143 the canons had made provision out of their prebends for the appointment of two clerks, who acted as readers during the offices and helped with routine administration. Crispin, the young clerk named in the early 1130s, came from the neighbourhood of Waltham and was a nephew of Richard of Hastings, a later Master of the Temple in London.[6]

The church with its Holy Cross was closely bound up with the local community. The nave was the parish church; lay people attended the daytime offices there, and pilgrims came from both the locality and further afield to pray at the altar of the Holy Cross. Like other consecrated, stone buildings, it was a place of refuge in times of war and disorder. The account of the attempt of Flemish mercenaries to steal the personal belongings of the townspeople brought there for protection[7] is reminiscent of Orderic Vitalis's description of the church at Carenton, where Henry I and his men heard mass during his 1105 campaign in Normandy.[8] Both churches were so crammed with chests and boxes that it was as difficult for the thieves at Waltham to find a way out with their loot as it was for the king and his household knights at Carenton to make their way to the altar rail. Whether or not the lives of the canons became lax and the community grew more worldly later in the

---

[1] See below, cap. 20.
[2] See below, cap. 26.
[3] Cf. *CCM* vi. 237–40 for the duties of the sacristan at Monte Cassino. At Afflighem (ibid., pp. 186–90) and probably in other houses the *custos ecclesie* helped the sacristan and did not hold two offices.
[4] See below, cap. 33.
[5] *Statuta Petri Venerabilis* (*CCM* vi. 99–100).
[6] See below, cap. 27.
[7] See below, cap. 31.
[8] Orderic, vi. 60.

century, the canons evidently performed the offices with dignity and were respected locally by both magnates and peasants up to the time the Chronicle comes to an end in 1144.

THE CHRONICLE AND ITS SOURCES

The Chronicle, which survives only in thirteenth- and fourteenth-century copies, begins without an introduction, and there is no indication whether it ever had one. Since the last section consists of miracles it was possibly left open-ended, so that more miracles might be added if and when they occurred. The pattern is not uncommon in foundation histories, except that whereas many miracle collections were intended to prepare the way for the canonization of a holy abbot or other confessor, Waltham's collection aimed rather at deflecting any attempt to promote a cult of King Harold while continuing to attract pilgrims.

The chronicler wrote shortly after the dissolution of the secular college in 1177,[1] and appears to have been the first historian of the house. But if he had no earlier annals, he certainly consulted the available archives; he had before him the foundation charter of King Edward and at least one charter, now lost, of William Rufus, restoring to the canons the vill of Waltham which had been given to Walcher, bishop of Durham.[2] He used too a list of valuables copied by Master Adelard into the chapter book,[3] a list of treasures taken by Rufus,[4] and a written account of an early lawsuit.[5] Details of the division of the prebends and the food allowances of the canons may have come also in part from written records. Otherwise he relied on oral sources of various kinds and his own recollections. The earliest traditions had already gathered a good many of the trappings of legend, for which the region of Montacute was a fertile source. They appear to be stories repeated at Waltham from an early date. On the other hand, it would be interesting to know when the author first came across the story (which he claimed to have both heard and read) of the ring given to St John and restored

[1] It was written before 1189, the year of the death of William de Mandeville, who was still alive when the chronicler wrote.
[2] See below, cap. 22.
[3] See below, cap. 17.
[4] See below, cap. 22.
[5] See below, cap. 24.

to King Edward by pilgrims. It is different in many details from the version known to Osbert of Clare and Ailred of Rievaulx, but may not have been current at Waltham before the development of Edward's cult in the twelfth century.[1]

By about 1060 information from the children of alleged eye-witnesses begins, shortly to be followed by reports of eye-witnesses themselves. The chronicler's own recollections begin about 1124. Both he and his informants may have attributed some customs they knew in their own time to an earlier date; he imagined anachronistically that Tovi had been a belted knight. There are hints, often between the lines, of the ways in which the lives of the canons may have become less strict, but it is not possible to chart the changes precisely. Again, what the author wrote about the appearance of Harold's church at Waltham may have been coloured by his familiarity with the later church in which so much of his daily life was spent.

Nevertheless the degree of detachment he achieved is remarkable. His whole life had been spent in a church founded by a Saxon king and taken over by his Norman conquerors. He owed to the wife of the Norman, Henry I, the prebend of which he was finally deprived by that king's grandson, Henry II. In spite of this he kept a balance between admiration for King Harold and respect for King William I; he regretted the end of the community that had nurtured him, while accepting that, being sinful, he himself was not without some responsibility. His gratitude for what he had enjoyed is evident in the loving care with which he explored all available sources, and worked to preserve the traditions of his church so that they might be respected by the canons of a different order who were the heirs of Waltham.

The first chapters deal with the visions of a smith living at Montacute, which led to the discovery of the Holy Cross on the hilltop there. This is a typical miracle story, describing how a mysterious figure appeared three times in visions to the smith, each time more insistent, before he could be persuaded to summon all the parishioners to dig on the hill in search of the cross there. As in other similar stories, when the figure appeared in the third vision he seized the smith's arm with a grip fierce enough to

---

[1] For other versions of the legend of the ring and the cult of King Edward, see Barlow, *VER*, pp. xxxv–xxxvii.

leave the imprint of nails as proof of the visitation.[1] The search revealed a figure of the crucified Christ, carved out of a hard black stone, possibly Tournai marble:[2] the Latin wording seems to apply to the figure itself (*imago Christi*), and any wooden cross to which it would once have been attached is not explicitly mentioned, though the smith had been told to look for a cross (*crucem sancte domini passionis signum*).[3] There was also a smaller crucifix, an ancient bell like an ox-bell, and a book of the Gospels, called the Black Book.[4] For all this part of the chronicle the author depended on oral accounts handed down in the community. Some of these, however, related to objects cherished by them, including the gospel book as well as the crucified figure itself.[5]

With the mention of Tovi, legend touches history. At the time of the discovery he was occupied with the king's business in some other part of the realm, where indeed his duties as staller and

[1] See below, caps. 1–7. Stories of visions three times repeated go back to the calling of Samuel (1 Kings (1 Sam.) 3: 4–10). There is a particularly close parallel in the vision of a smith described by Lantfred of Winchester in *Sancti Swithuni Wintoniensis episcopi translatio et miracula auctore Lantfredo monacho Wintoniensi*, ed. E. P. Sauvage, *Analecta Bollandiana*, iv (1885), 367–410 (cap. 1). By the 12th cent. the numerous accounts of *inventiones* of relics had become stereotyped and the legend of Waltham follows a standard pattern. See Patrick J. Geary, '*Furta Sacra*': *Thefts of Relics in the Central Middle Ages* (Princeton, NJ, 1978), pp. 13–14.

[2] The blue lias limestone from Somerset, which takes a fine polish and has sometimes been mistaken for Tournai marble, was later used at Glastonbury, Sherborne, and Salisbury (see *English Romanesque Art 1066–1200*, Catalogue of the Exhibition at Hayward Gallery, Arts Council of Great Britain, London, 1984, no. 149a; R. A. Stalley, 'A twelfth-century patron of architecture. A study of the buildings erected by Roger, bishop of Salisbury, 1102–1139', *JBAA* xxxiv (1971), 62–83, at p. 75 n. 1). If it was used here, the figure would probably have been carved in the west country. The date is early for the importation of Tournai marble.

[3] For the legend of the finding of the True Cross, which was one of the earliest of the *inventio* stories, see above, p. xiv n. 3. There was, however, no connection between the True Cross and the *imago Christi* found at Montacute, though this passage has sometimes been misinterpreted in that sense (cf. Gransden, *Historical Writing*, p. 273).

[4] BL Harley MS 3776, fos. 33^r–35^v contains a list of relics and treasures given to Waltham. The list includes, besides the Holy Cross, 'liber etiam qui inuentus fuerat cum ipsa cruce qui et nigra dicitur, pro eo quod littera et parcamenum uilissima sint et antiquissima. . . . Tintinnabulum eciam humile ex antiquo opere cum eadem cruce inuentum' (Rogers, 'Waltham relic-list', p. 175).

[5] Two Saxon gospellers were in the possession of Waltham Abbey at the Dissolution; one may have been that discovered on this occasion, but either or both may have been given by Earl Harold. An inventory made in 1540 includes, 'A Gospeler of the Saxon Tongue, having thone syde plated with silver gilte, with ye ymage of Cryst. an other Gospeler of the Saxon Tonge, with the Crusifixe and Mary and John having a naked man holding up his hands of silver gilte' (printed W. Winters, *The History of the Ancient Parish of Waltham Abbey or Holy Cross* (Waltham Abbey, 1888), p. 138).

king's messenger might have taken him. He then took charge, and the legendary account of how the precious relics were carried to his estate at Waltham, after the oxen pulling the cart refused to travel anywhere else, follows. The description of the embellishment of the figure and the gifts of Tovi and his wife Gytha comes next. All these chapters continue to depend on oral tradition.

The author introduced written evidence when he was able to find any. The names of the vills given by Tovi could possibly have been found through reference to them in later charters.[1] A few written records became available from the time of Harold's foundation of the secular college. There was King Edward's charter itself, written partly at least in gold letters, which the chronicler had seen and from which he may have copied.[2] His account, based on the lost original, differs in places from the surviving cartulary copies, and suggests that he may have used an earlier draft. He used Master Adelard's list in the chapter book for the treasures and relics given by Harold. Another early written record, known only from the Chronicle, is of remarkable interest as an account of pre-Conquest legal proceedings. Very shortly after the foundation, four thieves who were robbing churches stole some of the precious silver vessels given to Waltham by Tovi and Gytha. After finding their way with difficulty across the marshes, they reached London and offered the vessels for sale to Theodoric the goldsmith. He at once recognized them as articles he himself had made for Waltham, and, after charging the men before witnesses with theft, had them sent back with the witnesses to Waltham. They were tried and condemned; one who admitted to being a clerk was branded on the face with the red-hot key of the church, and the others were sentenced to death. It is clearly an account of proceedings in a case in which thieves were caught red-handed, and it fell into the category of *furtum probatum et morte dignum*, the Old English *open þiefþ*.[3] The separate status of clerks at law was recognized in the Old English codes:[4] for serious crimes they were degraded and

---

[1] See below, cap. 12. The vills named are Waltham, *Chenlevedene*, Hitchin, Lambeth, Loughton, and Alderton, only some of which formed part of the later endowment of the secular canons. After 1060 they held only a small part of Waltham; Lambeth was temporarily lost and restored by King Edward; Hitchin was permanently lost, and the identity of *Chenlevedene* is uncertain. See below, pp. xxxix–xl.

[2] See below, cap. 18.

[3] Cf. *Leges Henrici Primi*, ed. L. J. Downer (Oxford, 1972), pp. 439–41.

[4] Cf. VIII Æthelred (1014), 26, 27 (F. Liebermann, *Die Gesetze der Angelsachsen*, Halle a. S., 1903–6, i. 266).

sometimes exiled, and branding would prevent a man from ever again escaping death by pleading clergy. Sometimes records of legal cases concerning property were preserved by being copied into service books.[1] This case may have been recorded in the same way, or in a separate schedule; the chance that took the thieves to the one man capable of recognizing the provenance of the stolen goods was regarded by the canons as miraculous and so worth recording.[2] The details are more precise and authentic than if they had depended on memory alone.

Up to and sometimes beyond the refoundation oral evidence was handed down through more than one person, like the description of great bowls of wine and mead set out at crossroads for all travellers when the church was dedicated.[3] From about 1066 the chronicler began to record stories told him as a child by old men who claimed to be reporting what they had seen with their own eyes. Chief among them was the old sacristan Turkill, who remembered Harold's visit to the church. The old men who said that they had seen and touched the wounds cutting into Harold's bones may have been recalling the original burial of the body in 1066; we are not told whether the body itself was actually examined during the later translations, and the coffin or other wrapping may not have been opened.[4]

For the twelfth century his own memories and those of his fellow canons are interwoven with accounts of the miracles witnessed in the church. He made the standard assertion that the miracles were all happenings he had either seen with his own eyes or heard from trustworthy eye-witnesses. For most, indeed, a rational explanation can be offered. The details they contain of the life of the community, the family connections of its benefactors, and the local disturbances during the anarchy of Stephen's reign incidentally give a special historical interest to the Chronicle. But for the author of the Chronicle the cross was more than a wonder-working relic; it was of the substance of Christ himself, for when Tovi's men tried to attach gold- and silver-plate to the image with studs the black stone oozed blood; and when Harold was about to depart

---

[1] See e.g. a record of a lawsuit in Herefordshire (1016–1035): Robertson, *AS Charters*, no. 78, trans. *EHD* i, no. 135.

[2] See below, cap. 24.

[3] See below, cap. 16.

[4] Some bodies, even of eminent people, were buried sewn into ox-skins, others in stone coffins; there are no details of Harold's burial.

for Hastings the image bowed its head in sorrow. In the last ten chapters of the Chronicle it is the figure on the cross which performs the miracles described, most of which occurred either before the author joined the college or when he was a young acolyte, but he accepted the stories, believed them implicitly, and honoured the cross with a deep devotion.

THE FOUNDATION CHARTER OF WALTHAM AND THE CHRONICLE

The writer of the Chronicle made use of Edward the Confessor's confirmation charter for Waltham, dated 1062, together with some oral traditions and at least one other written document, in his account of Harold's foundation and endowment of the secular college. In 1204 the royal charter of confirmation treasured by the canons was described in a list of relics and valuables at Waltham in these words: 'Carta quoque eiusdem regis [King Edward] huic ecclesie de confirmatione et adiectione quorundam possessionum antiquorum aureis litteris in pluribus locis scripta.' The chronicler had seen this document, which he described as 'carta . . . litteris aureis scripta'.[1] It has since been lost and is known only from later copies. Unfortunately Kemble printed it from a corrupt text (BL Cotton Tiberius C IX), and so helped to fuel attacks on its authenticity.[2] Better texts exist in a charter roll in the Public Record Office, edited by J. Conway Davies in *Cartae Antiquae*,[3] and in the still unprinted BL Harley 391, fos. 33ʳ–35ᵛ, which is substantially the same. Although the charter was regarded with suspicion by some historians, including F. M. Stenton and Tryggvi Oleson,[4] recent work by Simon Keynes has shown the insecure foundations for their criticism and pointed to some very good reasons for regarding it as substantially authentic.[5] Practices once considered alien to Anglo-Saxon usage are now known to have existed before

---

[1] BL Harley MS 3776, fos. 33ʳ–35ᵛ, and below, cap. 18.

[2] Kemble, no. 813.

[3] *Cartae Antiquae* PRS, pp. 34–8. A new edition of the charter is being prepared by C. R. Hart in his forthcoming edition of the charters of Barking Abbey.

[4] F. M. Stenton, *The Latin Charters of the Anglo-Saxon Period* (Oxford, 1955), pp. 86–7; Tryggvi J. Oleson, *The Witanagemot in the Reign of Edward the Confessor* (Toronto, 1955), p. 153.

[5] Keynes, 'Regenbald', pp. 200–9.

the Conquest: some names that appeared to be inaccurate were in fact garbled in the corrupt text, and the belief of Tryggvi Oleson that Bishop Ælfwold of Sherborne had died in 1058 and so could not have witnessed an authentic charter rests on flimsy evidence: Ælfwold is known to have been alive in 1059 and may have lived until 1062; if so Hereman may have remained at Ramsbury.

Much of the information given in the Chronicle corresponds with that in the confirmation charter. There are discrepancies, but if examined closely they do not invalidate the confirmation. Much can be explained by the fact that the chronicler was describing the foundation ceremony, which took place some two years before the charter recording the foundation and confirming both the first and some subsequent donations was written. Such a lapse of time was not uncommon in the slow business of monastic foundation.[1] The chronicler had certainly seen an earlier document of some kind, perhaps a draft charter, written down at the time and taken to the king as a basis for the formal document. This is clear from the appearance at the ceremony of Archbishop Cynesige of York, who died in December 1060 and was replaced by Ealdred; the chronicler cites the words of the anathema pronounced by Cynesige, which have not survived in any other document. There is no reason to suspect that either source wished to misrepresent the facts. The nature and contents of any earlier document can, however, only be conjectured. Moreover, even if the chronicler used some such record, his work was not written, as were some other chronicles, to preserve the details of a ceremony in order to obtain a charter, but to keep alive the memory of how the first college of Waltham was founded. He wrote a hundred years after the time of disorder, when some lands had been temporarily or permanently lost, and there was no longer any reason for him to record every detail of the endowment. His interest was in describing first the provision made by Harold for the prebends of the dean and canons, and then the ceremony attended by the king and court. In his account of the ceremony he added the names of two manors, Lambeth and Hitchin, which he said were the gift of King Edward.[2] If we compare the properties he named with those in the

---

[1] Cf. V. H. Galbraith, 'Monastic foundation charters of the eleventh and twelfth centuries', *Cambridge Historical Journal*, iv (1934), 205–22, at pp. 206–8.

[2] Both Lambeth and Hitchin are manors which the author had included among Tovi's gifts; if his statement was correct they must have been lost after Tovi's death. Only Lambeth was recovered later.

charter, it becomes apparent that almost all the discrepancies can be explained by the different purposes of the two records. The chronicler specifies the dean's portion of Paslow Hall, South Weald, Arlesey, and West Waltham; and the lands allocated to the prebends of the canons: Alderton, Woodford, Brickenden, Netteswell, Loughton, Upminster, and Debden, and in addition allowances of forty shillings to each canon for clothes, called 'shroudland payment' and fifteen acres in 'Northland' (which was in Waltham).[1] He may have taken these details from a separate record, or from his knowledge of how the prebends were organized in the twelfth century. Although he made no mention of Walter Hall or Nazeing, which are both named in the charter, the 1177 refoundation charter of Henry II specified that there was 'shroudland' in Nazeing and 'shoeland' at Walter Hall,[2] and the provision of clothing allowances from these two properties may have gone back to Harold's foundation. As for the chronicler's statement that Lambeth and Hitchin were given by King Edward, both are included in the charter list, where no distinction of donors is attempted. There are, however, doubts about the effectiveness of any gift of Hitchin; according to the Domesday inquest the whole of the great manor of Hitchin had been held by Earl Harold in 1066 and the canons of Waltham made no claim to any land there.[3] Two properties, Millo and Wormley, which are named in the charter, are not mentioned even indirectly by the author of the Chronicle. Millo was said by the Domesday jurors to have belonged to Waltham in 1066 by gift of King Edward;[4] possibly the king made a late substitution of Millo for Hitchin, even though the name of *Hicche* (Hitchin) was not deleted from the charter. As for Wormley, the canons' possession was never challenged, and it may have been a gift made after 1060 by someone other than Harold.[5]

There is a remarkably close correspondence between the witnesses named in the two sources, though variations which have

---

[1] See below, cap. 15.

[2] Calendared, Ransford, *Waltham Charters*, no. 26; printed, *Cartae Antiquae* PRS, no. 357.

[3] It was suggested by Seebohm that the 'Hicche' owned by Tovi might have been the two hides which belonged to the church of the manor and in 1086 formed the rectory manor (*VCH Herts*, iii. 8).

[4] *VCH Beds*., i. 227; *DB* i. 210b.

[5] The holding in Wormley was small; even after a number of other gifts had been received the property was valued in 1254 at less than £5 (Ransford, *Waltham Charters*, p. liv).

crept into the spelling of their names in the course of transcription have seemed to some historians to discredit the charter. In fact there are convincing explanations for the few discrepancies. Apart from the archbishops, the ecclesiastics and secular magnates correspond almost exactly.[1] The chaplains Peter and Baldwin, Wigod the king's butler, and Herding the queen's butler, who appear only in the charter, were all members of the royal household rather than the court. They may not have been present at the ceremony of consecration, or their names may have been omitted by the chronicler who was more concerned with the presence of great men. Swithgar, the scribe who wrote the charter for signing, would have had no role to play in the consecration. On that occasion the last witness was Raulin the chamberlain,[2] who did not sign the charter. Since he occupied an office whose duties included looking after the royal treasure and some documents he is likely to have been at Waltham and perhaps to have taken charge of any record written during the eight days of feasting and celebration. The most conspicuous difference is in the names of the archbishops; the Chronicle mentions Cynesige of York, adding that the archbishopric of Canterbury was vacant at the time. And the episcopal anathema pronounced by Cynesige is transcribed in

---

[1] The lay magnates in both sources are the earls Harold (assumed but not mentioned in the Chronicle list), Ælfgar, Tostig, Leofwine, and Gyrth; Asgar the staller, Robert (fitz Wimarc) the king's kinsman, Raulf the staller, Bondig the palace official, Esbern the king's kinsman, Regenbald the chancellor, the thegns Brihtric and Ælfstan; Adzur and Yfing the king's stewards, Godwine the queen's steward, the thegns Doddo, Ælfgar, Brixi, Æthelnoth, Esbern, Eadwig, Eadric, Æthelmund, Siward, Æthelwold, and Æthelwig. The bishops in both sources are: Ælfwold, bishop of Sherborne (written as *Ailnothus* in the Chronicle); Hereman, bishop of Ramsbury; Leofric, bishop of Exeter; William, bishop of London; Æthelmær, bishop of Elmham; Leofwine, bishop of Lichfield; Wulfwig, bishop of Dorchester; Ælfwine, bishop (? of Durham); Æthelric, bishop of Selsey; Walter, bishop of Hereford; and Giso, bishop of Wells (wrongly called 'of Cirencester' in the Chronicle). The abbots named in the charter are: Æthelnoth of Glastonbury, Ælfwine of Ramsey, Wulfric of Ely, Leofric of Peterborough, Leofstan of St Albans, Æthelwig of Evesham, Ordric of Abingdon, Æthelsige of St Augustine's Canterbury, Leofstan of Bury St Edmunds, Edmund of Pershore, and Sihtric of Tavistock. The list in the Chronicle corresponds almost exactly, allowing for some variations of spelling. Æthelsige (Canterbury) becomes *Elsinus*, and there is one apparent discrepancy as Wulfstan replaces Leofstan. This could be a reference to Wulfstan of Gloucester, but most probably in view of the general agreement between the two lists there was a slip in transcription and Leofstan was meant. For the identifications of individuals we are indebted to Simon Keynes; in one or two places they differ from those suggested by R. Ransford.

[2] Simon Keynes suggests that this may possibly be a slip for 'Hugelin' *camerarius* or *cubicularius*, who occurs in other charters of King Edward.

these words: 'Ego Ginsi Eboracensis archiepiscopus una cum fratribus consecrationi ecclesie assistentibus excommunicamus, et a liminibus sancte matris ecclesie sequestramus, et maledictione perpetua condempnamus omnes transgressores huius regie et consularis donationis et eorum et nostre confirmationis. Amen, in perpetuum fiat, fiat.'[1]

After Cynesige's death in December 1060 he was replaced by Ealdred, who witnessed the 1062 charter together with Stigand of Canterbury. The anathema in the charter reads: 'Nos autem archiepiscopi et episcopi ad hanc confirmationem congregati ex precepto domini nostri regis eiusdem hortatu excommunicamus et maledictione perpetua condempnamus omnes transgressores huius consularis donationis et regalis concessionis.' Archbishop Stigand's position was ambiguous at this time; he was a pluralist and had received his *pallium* in 1058 from Pope Benedict X, whose acts were annulled the following year. Although his appointment to Canterbury in 1052 was due to the influence of Earl Godwine, many churchmen regarded him with such suspicion that Harold may have chosen not to involve him in the actual consecration of Waltham.[2] The chronicler's information was evidently derived from a source in which the archbishopric of Canterbury was regarded as vacant because of the irregularity of Stigand's position. Stigand was, however, at court in 1062 and remained precariously in office until his deposition by William I in 1069. Thereafter Norman and Anglo-Norman writers consistently refused to acknowledge that he had ever taken part in any ceremony they wished to regard as authentic.[3]

The Chronicle should not, in fact, provoke any doubts about the authenticity of the charter. Instead it gives some hints of how the Waltham canon went about his work. He had access to some written records and had seen and taken some information from the royal charter, resplendent with its gold letters. Apparently he worked from notes, not from the charter itself, as there are variants

---

[1] The wording of the royal anathema is identical in the two sources, apart from a minor change in the order of the last three words (charter, 'pariter et coronam auferat'; Chronicle, 'auferat et coronam'). Scribes very frequently made such minor changes in transcribing, especially if they were accustomed to particular rhythmic patterns.

[2] For Stigand's position, see Brooks, *Early Church of Canterbury*, pp. 304–9.

[3] This is particularly striking in their treatment of the coronations of Harold and William the Conqueror; cf. Orderic, ii. 138 n. 1, 182–3; William of Poitiers, *Gesta Guillelmi ducis Normannorum et regis Anglorum*, ed. Raymonde Foreville (Paris, 1952), p. 221.

in the spelling of names. Also, in so far as the witnesses correspond, they are listed in the same order as in the charter, but he admitted to not remembering the sees of the various bishops, and when he attempted to assign a see to Giso he named 'Cirencester' (never the bishop's seat) instead of Wells. The names of Giso and Walter (of Hereford) must have come from the charter, since they were not consecrated until 1061; but the chronicler also used some other document, such as an earlier record of the consecration ceremony, which gave the wording of Cynesige's anathema. Some information about the witnesses came from memory or other unidentifiable sources; he described Doddo, who was merely *princeps* in the charter, as the closest kinsman of the king, and anachronistically he gave the title of *comes* to Robert (fitz Wimarc), whose earldom of Norfolk or East Anglia dated from after the Conquest. He may possibly have seen at a later date a list of the properties assigned to provide for the separate prebends. In addition, he gathered oral traditions and the recollections of what old men had been told by their fathers. These he wove into a narrative, which was commemorative not legal. By the time he wrote, the secular college had been dismantled and the possessions of the new abbey were secured by the charters of Henry II; he had no motive for attempting to copy word for word the first royal charter. He simply used it incidentally, to help his narrative and show the importance of Harold's foundation.

THE DEATH AND BURIAL OF HAROLD

The anonymous canon gives the best and earliest account of the Waltham version of the death and burial of the founder of his house.[1] He begins by describing Harold's visit to the church to pray on his way south from Stamford Bridge, embellishing it with a story of a miraculous sign of impending disaster, given when the figure of the crucified Christ bowed its head sorrowfully as Harold prostrated himself in prayer. In common with all the versions of the Anglo-Saxon Chronicle, he does not attempt to describe how or at what point in the ensuing battle Harold was killed: a reticence

---

[1] See below, caps. 20–1. There is a summary of the different versions of Harold's death and burial in Freeman, *Norman Conquest* (2nd edn., 1875), iii, Appendix, Notes MM, QQ, RR.

which may indicate that no one among the survivors from the battle was really sure of this, in spite of the legends circulating among the Normans. The concern of the canons was to recover the body of their patron and give it honourable burial in the place of his choice. The author names two canons who had been sent along with the non-combatants in Harold's retinue: Osgod Cnoppe and Æthelric Childemaister, so that if the worst happened they could bring back King Harold's body and the bodies of other benefactors of their church.

His story is that they begged Duke William for Harold's body and the duke, after first announcing his intention of founding a monastery where prayers for all the dead including Harold might be recited, finally gave way to their request, refused the gold that they offered, and granted them safe-conduct for their return journey. Because, however, it was impossible to distinguish Harold's body where it lay among the heaps of dead on the battlefield, Osgod went in search of Harold's concubine, Edith Swanneck, and after she had identified the corpse of her lord, brought it back to Waltham for honourable burial.

The accounts in the earliest Norman and French sources are almost all radically different. William of Poitiers, followed fairly closely by Orderic Vitalis, said that Harold's body, which was almost unrecognizable, was brought to the duke, who ordered William Malet to bury it on the sea-shore; and that Harold's mother begged in vain to have it and offered in return its weight in gold. Poitiers quoted a ducal jest, that the dead man might appropriately guard the sea shore.[1] The *Carmen de Hastingae proelio*, whatever its date, knew and recounted a similar story, with the added detail that the place of burial was to be on top of a cliff, and that an epitaph calling Harold the guardian of the shore was to be engraved on a stone. This description has prompted some commentators to recall the pagan rite, whereby a king took his stand on the tumulus of his predecessor.[2] William of Malmesbury, however, writing a generation later, preferred a mixed story nearer to the Waltham version: that the duke had surrendered the body to Harold's mother, refusing to accept the payment she offered, and that she had taken it to Waltham for burial.[3] The third version is

---

[1] *Gesta Guillelmi*, pp. 204–5; Orderic, ii. 178–80.
[2] *Carmen*, vv. 572–92 (pp. 36–8), and pp. xliii–xliv.
[3] *Gesta Regum*, ii. 304–7.

later and legendary: that Harold had escaped alive from the battle and, after various wanderings, had ended his days as a penitent hermit in a cell near Chester.[1] It remained only for the author of the *Vita Haroldi*, providing a legend appropriate for Henry II's new royal house of regular canons at Waltham in the early thirteenth century, to take flight from all reality with increasing ingenuity. Harold, the *Vita* claimed, had escaped alive; he had never been buried at Waltham and, though the secular canons had believed that they had his body, Edith Swan-neck had made a mistake.[2]

Freeman, while rejecting the survival legends, tried to find a compromise between the earlier versions.[3] He suggested that the Waltham version was true in all but chronology; the body had first been buried by William Malet on the sea-shore, and some time later the canons had successfully pleaded to have it translated to Waltham. Yet a good case could be made for the substantial truth of the original Waltham version. Duke William had come to England claiming to be the just successor of King Edward, designated by him and approved by the pope. In the first months after establishing his rule he stressed his legitimacy, but did not refuse the dead Harold the title of king.[4] He was no pagan conqueror standing on the tumulus of his predecessor, but a Christian king claiming what he held to be his lawful inheritance, after a God-given victory in battle. It is not really conceivable that he would have refused his defeated enemy the kind of Christian burial that he himself hoped in due course to be given in his own abbey at Caen. William of Poitiers was writing a rhetorical panegyric, and the *Carmen* was an epic using all the literary conventions of its genre. Orderic accepted the authority of William of Poitiers current in Normandy, whereas William of Malmesbury used his sober judgement. As for the survival myth, it is one that constantly crops up in all periods.[5] The total rejection by the Augustinian canons of the authenticity of the body buried at Waltham can be explained by a wish to promote the status of the new foundation,

---

[1] For the legends, see Freeman, *Norman Conquest*, iii. 514–16, 785–7.

[2] *Vita Haroldi*, pp. 79–86.

[3] Freeman, *Norman Conquest*, iii. 508–14, 517–20, 781–5.

[4] See V. H. Galbraith, *Domesday Book: Its Place in Administrative History* (Oxford, 1974), pp. 175–83; George Garnett, 'Coronation and propaganda: implications of the Norman claim to the throne of England in 1066', *TRHS*, 5th ser., xxxvi (1986), 91–116, at p. 99.

[5] Cf. Margaret Ashdown, 'An Icelandic account of the survival of Harold Godwinson', *The Anglo-Saxons*, ed. P. Clemoes (London, 1959), pp. 112–36.

patronized by the royal line that had supplanted Harold, and a wish at all costs to avoid the tomb becoming the centre for a seditious cult. Archbishop Hubert Walter's firm action in suppressing the incipient cult of William Longbeard, who was executed in 1196,[1] may have been an added incentive in the late twelfth century to leave no room for a politically dangerous cult at Waltham. The *De inventione*, however, unlike the *Vita Haroldi*, recorded the older, more reliable Waltham traditions, and there is much in it which is both plausible and convincing.

THE CHRONICLE AND THE *VITA HAROLDI*

The Chronicle was little known in the middle ages outside Waltham. About thirty years after it was written it was used by the author of the *Vita Haroldi*, a work commissioned by the abbot of the Augustinian house[2] partly at least to prevent the growth of any seditious cult at Harold's supposed tomb. The author was probably not one of the canons, but a clerk loosely associated with the abbey. In welcoming their scrutiny of his work and deferring to their greater literary skill he acknowledges that there is no lack of men 'in your holy band' (*cetui sanctitatis vestre*) who could polish, prune, and adorn what he had written; and he frequently uses the second person plural pronoun or possessive adjective (*vestri*) when addressing them, as though he is outside the community.[3]

He built his story around existing legends of Harold's survival, which took various forms. In one, which was embodied in the Icelandic saga *Heming Aslakkson*, Harold was said to have been found wounded on the battlefield by a cottar and his wife, and to have lived for three more years in a hermitage at Canterbury. Other sagas recorded in various ways his rescue, miscellaneous adventures, and final retirement to a hermitage.[4] Gervase of Tilbury recognized the existence of the survival story when he wrote 'there is still doubt whether Harold fled or fell in the battle'.[5] The author of the *De inventione* knew and rejected the survival legends.[6] The *Vita Haroldi*, however, gave free rein to the fancy of

---

[1] Benedicta Ward, *Miracles and the Medieval Mind* (London, rev. edn., 1987), pp. 130–1.

[2] *Vita Haroldi*, pp. 4, 104.   [3] *Vita Haroldi*, p. 6.

[4] Margaret Ashdown, 'An Icelandic account', pp. 122, 128, 129.

[5] Freeman, *Norman Conquest*, iii. 785.   [6] See below, cap. 21.

its author and provided Harold with a brief stay in a hermitage at Dover, an adventurous later life, and a final retirement to spend ten years in another hermitage at Chester, where he confessed to his true identity.

There is little doubt that this writer knew of the Chronicle of Waltham as he refers to the discovery of the Holy Cross on the top of a hill, commenting that nobody knew who had conveyed it or hidden it there. Its conveyance 'one hundred and twenty miles' by oxen to Waltham is mentioned, as is the miracle of the blood oozing from the image when men tried to nail silver plate to it.[1] Harold's experience before the cross just prior to his march to Hastings when the image bowed its head is related, though the miracle is portrayed more graphically than in the Chronicle. Yet the author appears to have used the Chronicle selectively to suit his purpose, possibly writing from memory some time after reading it, for no mention is made of Montacute, or indeed of Tovi's part in the foundation of the original church. In fact he contends that William the Conqueror had the story of the cross written to palliate his own crimes against the church.[2] These crimes, according to the author, consisted of the transference to Normandy of a host of precious altars, books, candelabras, crosses, vestments, and sacred vessels, all of which recall the chronicler's list of items said to have been transferred to Normandy by William Rufus.

The *Vita* has more to say about Adelard, or Ailard, as his name is spelt. Described as an educator and physician he is said to have been sent to England by the German emperor when he learned that the efforts of Harold's own personal physicians had failed to heal him of a paralysis with which he had been afflicted. When Adelard found that his own skill was of no avail he persuaded Harold to pray before the cross and make a vow to it. Harold was healed, and out of gratitude he is said to have founded a new church at Waltham and established schools to operate under the direction of Master Adelard, to have proceeded swiftly with building works in order to raise walls, lofty columns, and interlacing arcades, and to have constructed a roof lined with lead. The author records that he increased the number of clergy from the two already existing to twelve, this being the only reference to the church already in existence.[3]

---

[1] *Vita Haroldi*, pp. 59, 161.   [2] Ibid., pp. 24–5, 124–5.
[3] Ibid., pp. 18–23, 118–23.

The story of Edith Swan-neck's (Swanneshals') visit to the battlefield is also related. She is said to have been more fitted for the task than any other because she had been frequently present in the secret places of his chamber ('utpote quam thalami ipsius secretis liberius interfuisse constaret'); the same sentiment is expressed in the Chronicle except in quite different words: 'ad ulteriora intima secretorum admissa'. In the *Vita*, however, her search meets with no success, and when she cannot distinguish Harold's body from others she chooses another mangled corpse to satisfy the expectations of those who have sent her: no mention is made of the two canons said by the author of the Chronicle to have accompanied her.[1]

The author of the *Vita* condemned 'the lies' of historians like William of Malmesbury, who had written that Harold was buried at Waltham. He offered instead unnamed or unacceptable authorities in support of the legends that he favoured.[2] Much depended on the stories of an anonymous hermit, and on the account said to have been given to Abbot Walter over a hundred years after the battle of Hastings by Harold's younger brother Gyrth, also said to have survived the battle. Fortunately the fanciful garbling of the Waltham legends in the *Vita Haroldi* did not persuade the canons to forget the older history of their house. The *De inventione* was copied at least twice in the abbey during the middle ages, and so was preserved for later readers after the original had been lost.[3]

THE MANUSCRIPTS AND EDITIONS

The text of the Waltham Chronicle is preserved in two manuscripts in the British Library, Cotton Julius D. VI, fos. 73–121 and Harley 3776, fos. 45ᵛ–62. In addition, there is a manuscript in a seventeenth-century hand, Harley 692, which is a copy of the Cotton MS. This is of use only to the extent that it provides

---

[1] *Vita Haroldi*, pp. 84, 188; see below, cap. 21.

[2] Ibid., pp. 80, 184–5.

[3] See below, pp. xlix–lii. One aim of the compiler of the Harleian volume was to provide a complete history of the early years of the house for interested readers. He included in his collection the *Vita Haroldi*, the *De inventione*, and a short chronicle which he prefaced with the words 'Ista que secuntur videlicet de Regibus Knouto, Hardecnouto et Haroldo deficiunt in libro de Invencione Crucis nostre de Waltham. Et ideo hic inseruntur ad instruccionem et solamen legere volencium ut habetur in cronicis nostris' (Harley MS 3776, fo. 25).

another opinion on any difficulties that occur in the earlier manuscript. The text of this present edition is based upon the Cotton manuscript, though this has been collated with Harley 3776, and reference has been made to Harley 692.

1. *The Cotton Manuscript*

The manuscript of the Waltham Chronicle is contained in a small quarto volume of 182 folios comprising seven articles in minuscule script. The pages of the manuscript are approximately 180 × 130 mm. The frame-ruling has double bounding lines, the outer frame being approximately 120 × 85 mm, and the inner frame containing the writing approximately 120 × 77 mm. Both the vertical and horizontal bounding lines run to the edge of the folio and this includes double ruling for the top and bottom line. Although this scribe is using a frame-ruling to contain the text (the *mise-en-page* system which appeared in the thirteenth century)[1] he has nevertheless continued to place his text above the top line, perhaps implying that he is used to working in an earlier tradition. His tendency throughout the work to cross the Tironian 'et' is a feature which increases during the thirteenth century, and the embellishment of ascenders on the top line of some pages suggests a date well into the thirteenth century, perhaps during the transitional period of *c.* 1210–30 and towards the latter part of this spectrum rather than earlier.

Each chapter begins with pen-flourished initials in red and blue, and these as well as the text hand, which is an early example of *Littera Gothica textualis semiquadrata* (1180–1230),[2] are of an acceptable quality. There are no chapter headings as such in this MS as there are in Harley 3776. These are contained in a chapter-list which precedes the Chronicle, and it is from this that the chapter headings of this present edition are extracted, the differences with the Harleian headings being noted in the apparatus. The hand of the chapter-list is virtually contemporary: however, there are more cursive features and forking of ascenders, which would suggest that this scribe may have had more of a background

[1] See N. R. Ker, 'From "Above top line" to "Below top line": a change in scribal practice', *Celtica*, v (1960), 13–16; repr. in id., *Books, Collectors and Libraries: Studies in the Medieval Heritage* (London and Ronceverte, n.d.), pp. 71–4.

[2] See Michelle P. Brown, *A Guide to Western Historical Scripts from Antiquity to 1600* (London, The British Library, 1990), p. 86.

of charter production in which these features are more common; he also observes the anachronism of placing his text above the top line despite the frame-ruling provided.

There are marginal annotations of varying periods throughout the manuscript, and five different hands appear to have been at work. At the foot of the first page of the text (fo. 75) the title of the work is recorded in a bastard *Anglicana* script, a textualis hand with significant *cursiva Anglicana* features, for example the forking of ascenders, putting it in the early fourteenth century. On fo. 79ᵛ there is a marginal annotation in metalpoint of fourteenth-century date, and there are occasional Cottonian marginal notes throughout. Manicula appear only twice in the MS, on fos. 88ᵛ and 94, this scribe favouring a somewhat extended finger. In the former case the reader's attention is being drawn to a passage describing the character of Earl Harold, and in the latter case to a passage relating the plan to divide the wood of the True Cross and bury one half for safe-keeping.

There is considerable water-staining throughout the MS, but this has not obliterated the script, which is of a high carbon lamp-black ink and very clear throughout. The reverse of fo. 122 is discoloured, indicating that it has probably acted as the outer cover for the MS before it was bound in this volume.

The accompanying texts are of fourteenth-century date but do not appear to have been incorporated with the Waltham MS until the late sixteenth or seventeenth century when the contents list was added and the volume refoliated. They comprise the final part of a history by John Pike of the kings of England up to the kings of the Saxons, Danes, and Normans to the year 1322 (fo. 1); excerpts from Marianus Scotus, Roger Howden, and William of Malmesbury on the right of the English king to territory in Scotland (fo. 67); two lives of St Edmund of Canterbury (fos. 123 and 161ᵛ); prayers from the Hours of the Blessed Virgin Mary which St Edmund used to say (fo. 156ᵛ); and a brief extract about the marriage of the father and mother of St Thomas the Martyr.

2. *Harley 3776*

This manuscript was written, probably in the scriptorium of the abbey, a century later than the Cotton manuscript. Its pages measure 260 × 200 mm, and the writing is contained within a

frame-ruling measuring 205 × 150 mm. The script is fourteenth-century *Gothica textualis quadrata*. Throughout the manuscript chapters begin with pen-flourished initials in red and blue with lavender adornment filling in the quatrefoil panels and adorning the margin, on two folios (45ᵛ and 49ᵛ) incorporating faces. The initial capitals of the chapter-list are blue and red alternately. In the left-hand margin of fo. 51ᵛ, alongside cap. 16, is a sketch of architectural columns showing the ornamented capitals, bases, and arches mentioned in the text. This and some of the marginal annotations may well be in the hand of Lord William Howard who probably owned the manuscript in the early seventeenth century, though there are contemporary fourteenth-century glosses in red, and manicula on several folios. There is internal evidence that the manuscript cannot be before 1345, as fos. 38–39ᵛ contain a poetic lament, in an original hand, on the death of the ninth abbot of Waltham, Richard of Hertford, who died in 1345.

Harley 3776, except for a few articles, was originally bound with Harley 3766, both volumes having been acquired by Humphrey Wanley, the Earl of Oxford's librarian, between 1720 and 1722.[1] Consecutive medieval numeration and foliation of the contents occur in both volumes, each article being signified by a large arabic numeral and the folios by smaller arabic numerals. Harley 3776 contains articles 1–8, and 3766 articles 9–16.

The text of the Waltham Chronicle ends on fo. 62, and is followed immediately (fos. 62–63ᵛ) by three verses in the same hand (see below, Appendix II). They may have been composed by the author of the Chronicle, and express the same sorrow for the death of Harold and the same hope that the new community of Augustinian canons will respect the old traditions. The lament for Harold must have been written before the new community attempted to question whether Harold's body lay at Waltham.[2]

Amongst the more important of the miscellaneous articles in Harley 3776 is the only extant copy of the *Vita Haroldi* (fos. 1–24ᵛ). The fifth article comprises lists of the relics given to Waltham by King Harold and others, the first of these lists being in hexameters and the others in prose. Another article, again in verse, summarizes the amenities enjoyed at Waltham, and this is followed by a

---

[1] For the history of the MS, see *British Museum Quarterly*, vii (4 May 1933).
[2] See above, pp. xliii–xlvi.

series of elegiac couplets or hexameters on the abbots of Waltham from Walter of Gaunt to the ninth abbot.

The article concludes with a table of 38 capitula on a new treatise. The first 28 leaves of this treatise are lost, but the 29th is fo. 1 of Harley 3766. The treatise is believed to have been copied from the *Liber Niger* mentioned in the Waltham Chronicle as having been found with the holy cross at Montacute.

3. *Harley 692*

This is a codex of manuscripts on paper. It comprises sixteen articles all written by one hand in a late cursive 'secretary' script of the seventeenth century. The last item in the manuscript was copied by this hand from an exemplar written by John Jocelyn (1529–1603), secretary to Archbishop Parker, in the Cotton collection. The compilation of this volume would therefore post-date Jocelyn's work. The first article is a copy of the Cotton manuscript of the Waltham Chronicle. Most significant amongst the other articles are a Life of St Edmund of Canterbury, a history of England between the years 854–1399 written by Simon Rawley, and an account of the churches founded in England before the arrival of the Normans.

The first printed edition of the whole Chronicle appears to be that of William Stubbs produced in 1861, though caps. 14–22 were printed in Francisque Michel's *Chroniques anglo-normandes* (Rouen, 1836), ii. 223–54. Caps. 1–22 are printed by J. A. Giles in his *Original Lives of Anglo-Saxons and Others who lived before the Conquest* (Caxton Society, 1854), pp. 280–307.

This present edition is the first to carry a translation as well as a text. The Cotton and the Harley 3776 manuscripts are both inconsistent in their spelling, especially of *c*s and *t*s, though Harley prefers *c* to *t* in words like *excusacionis*, *affluencie*, *evidencia* and *negociis*, whereas the Cotton scribe prefers *t*, as in *excusationis*, and his spelling has been adopted here. The Harley manuscript sometimes uses *s* instead of *c* in words like *senserat* (for *censerat*) and *obsecatione* (for *obcecatione*), a not uncommon medieval usage, but the *c*-spelling of the Cotton manuscript has been preferred in this edition. Scribal errors which make nonsense, especially when the

other manuscript clarifies the reading, have not been noted. In his edition Stubbs substituted classical orthography for medieval, but this edition returns to the medieval spelling, and the consonantal *u* of the manuscript has been reinstated in accord with OMT practice. The only liberty taken with the text has been to use capitals for all proper names where the scribe has been inconsistent, writing sometimes, for example, 'Tovi le Prude', at others 'Tovi le prude' or even 'tovi le prude'. Stubbs's punctuation is peculiar at times, and difficult to justify: the text in this edition has therefore been completely repunctuated in order to convey with greater clarity the meaning of the original, especially as the obscurity of language is in places increased by the scattering of commas which Stubbs apparently thought necessary. The text has also been laid out in paragraphs to assist understanding.

ficare ceperat in loco siluestri. quod
nunc Waltham dicitur. locus scilicet
amenus. siluis uberrimis circumcinc-
t. fluuio prisuum uberrimo qui legia
dicitur. ornatus amenitate pratorum
fertilium decorus. londoniis satis p-
pinquus thamensi fluuio fluminie
predicto influente contiguus. decer-
nit iniuale benefiuum quod iam cepit amplion margine dilatare si ue-
lit ea deus: ad hec loca transmittere.
Mirabile dictu fide mirabilius. cum
in sonuiss; nomen Waltham. ilico o-
uit se plaustrum. ita ut magis plaustrum boues impellere: quam ipsos boues plaustrum trahere censeres. Gaudio perelluntur corda fidelium. et feli-
ci ducatu insequentes imaginem e-
ctificti: exultant successib; quos opera
tus est deus benefitio prestito Lau-

PLATE 1. BL MS Cotton Julius D. VI, fo. 83ᵛ; by permission of the British Library

PLATE 2. BL MS Harley 3776, fo. 47ᵛ; by permission of the British Library

THE
WALTHAM CHRONICLE

i. *Qualiter fabro preceptum est per uisionem ut sacerdos indicat parochianis ieiunium, montis cacumen ascendant, fodiant, et inueniant crucem.*

fo. 75^r Regnante Cnuto et Anglis imperante,[1] in loco qui dicitur Mons Acutus, quem Lutegaresberi[2] compatriote appellant, uitam agebat in opere fabrili uir magne simplicitatis et bone indolis, uir sine malitia timens Deum et recedens a malo,[3] quales diligit Deus et sancto respicit pietatis intuitu, inter mediocres conprouintialium cateruas bone existimationis et benigne[a] conuersationis. Cuius instituta uite et morum respiciens, dulcis ille et puritatis amator Iesus, qui archana prudentibus et sapientibus abscondita reuelat paruulis,[4] uoluit per ipsum thesaurum diu absconditum gentibus intimare, et humilium benignus amator humili precone humilitatis sue insignia detegere. Huius igitur cognita fidelitate et morum fo. 75^v uenustate, com|missa est ei cura amministrationis aque, ignis, et luminarium ecclesie parochialis[5] a sacerdote in eadem diuina celebrante, qui non solum opum habundans communium, uerum etiam[b] morum honestate precellens, et sanctitatis habitu mores informante, exemplar continentie[6] fuit sacerdotibus et formula uite.

Denique faber predictus, ille officialis ecclesie, cum nocte quadam membra sopori composuisset, fessus opere fabrili, ut assolet, qui scilicet labor indefessus quanto magis ossa concutit, et omnia membrorum liniamenta dissoluit, tanto uehementiorem sompni profundioris quietem incutit. Sompno itaque deditus uidet per sompnium, enimuero ut uerum fatear set per uisionem,[7] uenerandi decoris effigiem; quam intuitus quasi clara luce, tremefactus subito

---

^a bone *H*   ^b et *H*

---

[1] Cnut reigned 1016–35. A date as late as 1035 can be accepted on the assumption that the discovery occurred some years before Tovi's foundation of the church in 1042.

[2] Although the old name of Ludgersbury was replaced by Montacute after the Norman Conquest, it was known also to William of Malmesbury in the 12th cent. (Stephen C. Morland, *Glastonbury, Domesday and Related Studies* (Glastonbury Antiquarian Society, 1991), p. 121). The author of the Chronicle may have been familiar with the commanding hill, which he describes. He is the sole authority for the story that the Holy Cross was discovered at Montacute, a place which was nearly two hundred miles from Waltham, but was associated also with other legends, especially those connected with Joseph of Arimathea (cf. Valerie M. Lagorio, 'The evolving legend of St Joseph of Glastonbury', *Speculum*, xlvi (1971), 209–31).

[3] Cf. Job 1: 1.   [4] Cf. Matt. 11: 25.

1. *Instructions are given to a smith in a vision that the priest should declare a fast for his parishioners, and that they should climb to the top of a hill, dig, and find a cross.*

When Cnut was on the throne ruling the English,[1] there lived in a place called Montacute, which my fellow-countrymen called Ludgersbury,[2] a man who was a smith by trade. He was a very honest, good-natured and benevolent man who feared God and shunned evil,[3] one of the kind of men God loves with a holy regard for their piety. Amongst the ordinary people of his community he was highly esteemed and was of a kindly disposition. Observing his mode of life and character, sweet Jesus, the lover of purity, who reveals to babes things hidden from the learned and wise,[4] wished to make known to the people through this very man a treasure long hidden away; He who is the gracious lover of the humble desired to disclose through this humble messenger the emblem of His own humility. Because of his faithfulness and his virtuous life he was entrusted with the responsibility of looking after the water, the fire, and the lamps in the parish church[5] by the priest who celebrated divine services in the same church, a man much occupied in good works amongst the people as well as being a fine, upright man; in his holy life which shaped his character he was a pattern of continence[6] for priests, and a model of how to live.

One night this smith I have mentioned, this officer of the church, laid his limbs down to sleep exhausted as usual by the work of his trade; of course, the more his relentless toil shook his bones and relaxed all his muscles, the more surely did it induce a deep, restful sleep. So it was that when he was fast asleep he saw in a dream (in truth it was really a vision[7]) a figure of divine beauty. Gazing at it as if in bright daylight, he trembled at the sudden,

---

[5] Evidently he acted as sacristan in the parish church.

[6] In Cnut's reign celibacy was not required of the clergy; but this is one of a number of places where the author insists on the virtue of chastity by showing how a married layman could, by practising continence, be a model for the clergy.

[7] Visions could occur during sleep; although imaginative visions were thought to proceed sometimes from diabolical influence many were held to be divine revelations. Medieval vision literature is vast; for a useful calendar of some visions reported in contemporary sources see Peter Dinzelbacher, *Vision und Visionsliteratur im Mittelalter* (Monographien zur Geschichte des Mittelalters, xxiii, Stuttgart, 1981), pp. 13–17; and for definitions of the terms used ibid., pp. 45–50.

fo. 76ʳ insolito euentu, audiuit | dicentem: 'Summo mane cum sol mundo
illuxerit et euocauerint te debite amministrationes ecclesie, dic
sacerdoti diuine uoluntati placere, quatinus excitis undique
parochianis suis utriusque sexus, moneat paterna exhortatione
omnes se ieiuniorum, orationum, et confessionum ornamentis
uenustare, ut piorum applicatione studiorum digni inueniantur
celestium reuelatione munerum gratiam consequi: sicque ad
montis cacumen ordinata processione ascendentes, terram fodiant
donec diuini muneris exhibitione inueniant thesaurum a seculis
absconditum, crucem scilicet sancte Domini[a] passionis signum.'

ii. *Qualiter iterum apparuit fabro ymago increpans eum quia iniuncto non
obediuit mandato.*

Euigilans igitur uir ille animo uoluens quid uidisse per sompnium
fo. 76ᵛ sibi contigerit, aliquandiu confortatus quia uisione delec|tatus,
tandem quasi uana ymaginatione illusum se putans, nichili pendit
iussa complere. Elapso itaque temporis diuturniori spatio, iterum
quiescenti fabro apparuit per sompnium eadem imago, toruiori
quidem uultu, plus solito increpans et quadam facilitate obiurgans
cur iniuncto non obedisset mandato. Ad quam, cum pretenderet
excusationis formam, presbiterum[1] magni nominis et multarum
opulentiarum affluentie uirum, indignaturum huiuscemodi mandatum suscipere per tante humilitatis et pannose uilitatis per-
sonam, accepit responsum: 'Nichil quidem ueritus accedas ad
sacerdotem et iniuncta tibi mandata per ordinem pandas, quod si
ultra distuleris meritas inobedientie exsolues penas.' Hiis dictis
disparuit.

iii. *Qualiter consilio uxoris sue mandatum non expleuit.*

fo. 77ʳ Euocatus igitur a sompno simplex ille idiota, quales Deo placere
credimus, uxori sue que uiderat iam primo et secundo narrauit ex
ordine, set illa, ut assolent fatue mulieres, faciles quidem in dandis

---

[a] domice *H*

---

[1] *Presbyter* and *sacerdos* are used interchangeably in the Chronicle.

extraordinary event, and heard the figure say, 'When in the early morning the sun lights up the world and the necessary duties of the church call upon you, tell the priest that it is God's wish that he should summon all his parishioners from everywhere, both men and women, and urge them with fatherly exhortation to sanctify themselves with the fitting adornments of fasting, prayer and confession, so that they may be found worthy through these acts of pious devotion to receive God's grace in a revelation of heavenly gifts: they are to climb to the top of the hill in orderly procession and dig up the ground until, through a revelation of God's grace, they find a treasure hidden for generations, I mean a cross, the symbol of our Lord's holy passion.'

2. *The figure appeared again to the smith reproving him because he had not obeyed the commission laid upon him.*

After waking and reflecting upon what he had actually seen in the dream, the smith felt consoled for a while because of the pleasure he had experienced during the vision, but finally, thinking that he had been deceived by his own vain imaginings, he considered it of no importance to carry out the commands. After a long period of time had passed the same figure appeared to the smith in a dream when he was again resting; it looked more sternly at him and reproached him more severely than before, yet rebuked him with some indulgence for his neglectfulness in not obeying the command given him. In reply the smith made some sort of excuse that the priest[1] was a man of considerable reputation and very wealthy, and that he would consider it demeaning to carry out instructions of this sort conveyed by a person as humble and homespun as himself. He received the reply, 'You are to fear nothing, but to go to the priest and lay before him in detail the command I have given you. If you put this off any more you will be punished for your disobedience as you deserve.' So saying it disappeared.

3. *On the advice of his wife he did not carry out the orders.*

So that simple, uneducated man, one of the kind of men we believe God takes pleasure in, on awaking, told his wife in detail the events of the first, and then the second, of his dreams. She, however, being typical of foolish women who are quick to give thoughtless

indiscrete consiliis, sompniis fidem habere non censet, uisionem non discernens, quia non fuit ei datum desuper unde 'omne datum optimum et omne donum perfectum'.[1] Sicut ergo consueuit humana fragilitas dissuasioni in hiis que Dei sunt aurem facilem prebere, adquieuit uxori; inobediens quidem iniuncta non expleuit. Non tamen impune tulit, ut ipsa uexatio monimentum esset auditui, et asperitatem sentiret corripientis qui mansuetudinem contempserat dulciter ammonentis.

iiii. *Qualiter tertia uice ymago apparuit fabro et brachium eius strinxit.*

fo. 77ᵛ Apparens ei itaque tertio sancte deuotionis ymago, aspero quidem uultu, intentans minas, et minis aliquid formidolosum superaddens ex iniuncti dilatione precepti, nam brachium ipsius fabri manu apprehendens ita fortiter strinxit, ut unguium preacutorum uestigia manifestis apparerent uestigiis, et mouendis malleis minus apta foret aptitudo lacerti. Cui et dixit: 'Nisi asinino more lacessitus, stimulo urgente, non elegisti iniuncta tibi mandata peragere, nunc tandem quasi mancipium fustigatus obedias, et euidentia[2] signorum carni tue impressorum manifestare poteris, quod nostris habenda sit fides mandatis.'

Expergefactus igitur a sompno, tumᵃ terrore sompnii, tum acris instantia strictionis, currit ad ecclesiam trepidus quia pauebat fo. 78ʳ subsecuturos | deteriores euentus; quod uiderat primo, secundo, et tertio sacerdoti narrans, exarationes etiam unguium que facte fuerant ei in monimentum ⟨demonstrans⟩.ᵇ Cuius uerbis presbiter satis credulus humi protinus deuotus sternitur, lacrimarum ubertate et sinceri cordis deuotione orans ut secundum multitudinem miserationum gratie Dei que audierat rerum exitus probaret, nec peccatis exigentibus suis uel alienis fraudaretur executione tantorum bonorum, set ex perceptione presentium munerum firmior sit expectatio futurorum, et glorificaretur et innotesceret nomen Domini in secula seculorum.

ᵃ cum . . . cum *H*   ᵇ demonstrans, *suppl. ed.*

---

[1] James 1: 17.
[2] Frequently visions were repeated two or three times in vision narratives, and tangible proof was offered to convince the dreamer that he had not been deluded; cf. for example Peter Bartholomew's story of the Holy Lance, which he alleged had been revealed to him by St Andrew (*Gesta Francorum et aliorum Hierosolimitanorum*, ed. Rosalind Hill (NMT, 1962), pp. 59–60).

advice, did not think that any credence should be given to the dreams; she had not discerned that this was a vision, for that insight was not given to her from above, whence 'comes every good and every perfect gift'.[1] Accordingly, he fell prey to that common human failing of offering a ready ear to any who would turn us from the things of God, and he gave in to his wife. He was disobedient and failed to carry out the commands. But he did not go unpunished, for his conscience kept pricking him about what he had heard, and he who had despised the gentleness of one who had graciously admonished him was to feel his harsh grip.

4. *The figure appeared to the smith a third time and gripped his arm.*

That holy figure, therefore, appeared to him a third time, looking at him fiercely and uttering threats, and in addition to those threats it did something frightening because he had delayed carrying out the command, for grasping the smith's arm with its hand it gripped it with such force that it left the clear imprint of its sharp finger-nails and weakened the power of his arm for wielding the hammer. It then said to him, 'Because you have not been prodded like an ass or urged on with a goad you have chosen not to carry out the commission laid upon you, but now at last, chastised like a slave, do as I bid; you will be able to show the marks on your flesh as visible proof[2] that my commands must be believed.'

Waking from his sleep not only because he was terrified by the dream but also because of the pain from that fierce grip, he ran to the church trembling because he feared that worse punishment would follow. He told the priest what he had seen on the first, the second, and the third occasion, ⟨and showed⟩ the marks of the finger-nails which had been made as a warning to him. The priest was quite convinced by his words and instantly prostrated himself in prayer; with the devotion of a pure heart he prayed with many tears that, according to the multitude of God's gracious mercies future events would prove the truth of what he had heard, that neither his own sins nor those of others might stand in his way and deprive him of accomplishing such good works, that from his understanding of God's present favours his anticipation of future blessings might be all the stronger, and the name of the Lord be glorified and made known to all men for ever and ever.

v. *Qualiter sacerdos conuocauit parochianos.*

Surgens itaque et cum omni festinatione conuocans populum utriusque sexus, maiores et minores natu, monet ut pari uoto, unanimi
fo. 78ᵛ consensu, Domini misericordiam inuocarent quatinus | uisitet eos
in salutari suo[1] et adoptate promissionis, duce spiritu sancto,
gaudia producere dignetur: commonitorio etiam facto, paterno
desiderio, corde contrito et humiliato, cum lacrimarum ubertate
sic posse cacumina montis inuisere, ut peccatis non obstantibus
mereantur archanorum sibi promissorum solempnitate participes
effici.

Hoc iam solatio iocunditatis potiti, die constituto adest multitudo plebium, non solum indigenarum uerum etiam longe remo-
tarum partium, exultantium suis temporibus illustrari tam
singulari miraculo prouintiam,[2] unico dolore contriti quod in ulti-
mis tunc terre finibus degeret qui preerat prouintie, Toui le Prude[3]
dominus fundi.

vi. *Qualiter ascenduntᵃ Montem Acutum, fodiunt, inueniunt duas cruces,
nolam, et librum.*

fo. 79ʳ Ordinata igitur processione et omnibus preuise | dispositis, impo-
sita letania que sic incipit 'Humili prece et sincera deuotione',[4]
precedente fabro ueniunt ad locum sibi destinatum a Deo, ubi
facta oratione et uberrima a plebe lacrimarum effusione incipiunt
fodere, donec effossis .xl. cubitis[5] mire magnitudinis lapidem
reperiunt in cuius medio uisa est quasi fissura dehiscens. Amoto
itaque tanti lapidis ingenti obumbraculo non minus fletuum
ubertate quam manuum impulsione, quam magna multitudo
dulcedinis tue, Domine, quam ucusque absconderas diligentibus
te, ecce, repente apparuit oculis intuentium inestimabilis ymago

ᵃ ascenderunt *H*

---

[1] Cf. Ps. 105 (106): 4.
[2] *Provincia* was a word sometimes used of a former Anglo-Saxon kingdom that had
become a county; but here it probably has a more general sense of 'region'.
[3] For Tovi the Proud see above, pp. xv–xix.
[4] This metrical litany, originally composed by Hartmann of St Gallen, was incorporated in the *Romano-German Pontifical*, made at the church of St Alban in Mainz and
transmitted to England in the mid-11th cent. This passage provides important additional evidence of its dissemination in England. See *Le Pontifical romano-germanique du
dixième siècle*, ed. C. Vogel and R. Else, 3 vols. (Vatican City, 1963–72), iii. 123–6. On

5. *The priest called together his parishioners.*

The priest rose therefore, and with all haste summoned the people, men and women both young and old. He urged them to call upon the Lord's mercy in united prayer and singleness of mind that he might visit them with his salvation[1] and consider them worthy by the guidance of the Holy Spirit to experience the joys of the promised inheritance. Thus admonishing them with fatherly love and a humble and contrite heart, he prayed, with many tears, that they might be allowed to go to the top of the hill and, despite their sins, be worthy participants in the solemn revelation of the secrets promised to them.

On an appointed day, therefore, heartened by these words of encouragement, a large number of people gathered together composed not only of local inhabitants but also of those from distant parts. They all rejoiced that in their generation their own region[2] was being made famous by so singular a miracle. Their only regret was that the lord of the estate, Tovi the Proud, who exercised authority in the district,[3] was at that time busy in the most distant parts of the land.

6. *They climb Montacute, dig and find two crosses, a bell and a book.*

They made their way in an orderly procession, everyone in a pre-arranged place, using a set litany which begins 'With humble prayer and pure devotion'.[4] With the smith at the head they came to the place where God had directed them, and here, after a prayer and the shedding of many tears by the people, they began to dig until, at the depth of forty cubits,[5] they found a stone of incredible size in the middle of which there appeared, as it were, a gaping fissure. The mass of debris hiding the huge stone was removed as much by their copious tears as by the pressure of their hands. How great was the abundance of your kindness, O Lord, which you had concealed until then from those that loved you, for see, there suddenly appeared before the eyes of those gazing upon it an image of inestimable beauty of the crucified Savour, carved out of

Hartmann's metrical litany, see also M. Lapidge, *Anglo-Saxon Litanies of the Saints* (Henry Bradshaw Society, cvi, London, 1991), pp. 54–6.
[5] The expression 'forty cubits' implies that they dug to a very great depth.

decoris crucifixi saluatoris ex atro silice,[1] sic manuum extensione et omnium corporis liniamentorum compositione miro fabrili et

fo. 79ᵛ inaudito opere composita, ut ipsius summi artificis | manibus perpenderes[a] operatam; et sub dextro ipsius brachio alteram crucifixi effigiem modicam, in sinistra parte nolam[2] antiqui operis quales bestiarum collo applicare solet antiquitas, ne in desuetione insolescant.[3] Librum etiam cognomento Nigrum, textum[4] sicut uix perpendere possumus euangeliorum, quem usque hodie celebrem habet Walthamensis ecclesia propter multa que ipsi oculis nostris perspeximus miracula.

Hiis ita diuino nutu preostensis, tam ingentis nouitate miraculi uideres mentes attonitas, corda nutantia, Domini tamen nomen laudantia et dicentia 'Cantate Domino canticum nouum, quia fecit hodie nobiscum mirabilia. Quam terribilia sunt opera tua, Domine uirtutum, et nimis profunde sunt cogitationes tue.'[5] Quidam

fo. 80ʳ retrahunt gressum, | reminiscentes preteritorum commissorum, pars pugnis pectora tundit, quidam stupefacti nouitate miraculi, quasi extra se facti, quid agant nesciunt. Stupor enim ingens inuaserat omnes. Que tunc lacrimarum uberrima flumina per facies uiduarum, uirginum, necnon et continentium, ut imaginarie offerentur earum lacrime quibus dictum est, 'Filie Ierusalem, nolite flere, etc.'[6] Illis quidem iusta lamentandi causa, que posteritati sue dampnationem comparauerant[b] dicentes, 'Sanguis eius super nos et super filios nostros'.[7] Nostris uero iusta letandi causa, que pretioso ipsius redempte sanguine, inebriate 'ubertate domus sue et torrente uoluptatis potate',[8] quanto flebant uberius, tanto securius, quia huiusmodi fletum sequitur sine intermissione letitia.

---

[a] perpendas C; perpenderes H   [b] conperauerunt *with later interlin. emend. to* comparauerunt C

---

[1] The exact meaning of *silex*, used of a hard stone, is uncertain: see above, p. xxxv and n. 2.

[2] See above, p. xxxv.

[3] This bell and the black book were still preserved among the relics of the church at the beginning of the 13th cent.; see above, p. xxxv. As it was of base metal, it was not included in the Dissolution inventory ('Inventory of Waltham Holy Cross', ed. M. E. C. Walcott, *TEAS* v (1873), 257–64). Since it was described as rough in the relic list it may have been the kind worn by cattle to prevent them wandering; alternatively, Nicholas Rogers, 'Waltham relic-list', p. 161, suggests that it was possibly a Celtic hand-bell.

[4] It is not clear whether the reference is to one or two books. The extracts from the *Liber Niger* copied in Harley 3766 were from a legendary, not a gospel book. Nicholas

black stone,[1] with hands outstretched and every lineament of the body reproduced with such wonderful skill and unprecedented workmanship that you might think it the work of the Supreme Craftsman himself. Under its right arm lay another small crucifix, and on the left side there was a bell[2] of ancient workmanship such as men of old used to fasten to the necks of animals to prevent them going astray when not in harness.[3] There was also a book called the Black Book, a text[4] of the Gospels such as we can scarcely over-value, and to this day the church at Waltham holds it in honour because of the many miracles which we ourselves have witnessed with our own eyes.

As these things were revealed according to God's will, so you could see that the people's minds were struck by the extraordinary nature of so great a miracle and that their hearts almost failed them. Yet they praised the name of the Lord, saying 'O sing unto the Lord a new song, for he has done marvellous things with us today; how terrible are thy works, O Lord of all goodness, how fathomless are thy thoughts!'[5] Some returned home, remembering their past sins, others beat their breasts with their fists, still others, struck by the wonder of the miracle, as if out of their senses, did not know what to do. A great sense of wonder had come upon them all. What floods of tears then streamed down the faces of widows, of maidens, and also of those vowed to continence, so that one could visualize the tears that were shed by the women to whom it was said 'Daughters of Jerusalem, do not weep . . .'![6] Indeed, those people of old had good reason to weep, for they had ensured condemnation for their descendants when they said 'His blood be upon us and our children'.[7] But our people had good reason to rejoice, for they had been redeemed by the precious blood of the Lord himself, overjoyed with the 'riches of His temple, and had drunk of the river of His pleasure';[8] the more they wept the less fearful they became, for tears of this sort are followed by joys for evermore.

Rogers, 'Waltham relic-list', p. 161, suggests that it may have been a composite volume. Waltham certainly possessed two Saxon gospellers, but they may have formed part of Earl Harold's endowment; see above, p. xxi. The relic-list has also been published by Paul Gerhard Schmidt, 'König Harold und die Reliquien von Waltham Abbey', *Anglo-Saxonica*, ed. K. R. Grinda and C.-D. Wetzel (Munich, 1993), pp. 75–90.

[5] Ps. 97 (98): 1; 91: 6 (92: 5).   [6] Cf. Luke 23: 28.
[7] Matt. 27: 25.   [8] Ps. 35: 9 (36: 8).

vii. *Qualiter mittitur pro domino feodi,*[1] *scilicet Thoui le Prude.*

fo. 80^v Cum igitur nullus se censeret dignum tantum manibus contingere thesaurum, tentoriis circumuallare propter aeris intemperiem et obseruationis cautelam placuit locum, et utriusque sexus personas deputare religiosas, qui uigiliarum excubias deuotis agerent obsequiis donec mirabilem rei euentum domino fundi Toui le Prude qui totius Anglie post regem primus, stallere,[2] uexillifer regis, monarchiam gubernabat, nuntiarent.

Ille tunc in remotis Anglie partibus degebat, regiis implicitus negotiis, secundus a rege, sicut qui pre ceteris terre magnatibus curam omnium gerebat et regi proximus in consiliis et precipuis regni causis assistebat. Audita itaque tanta exultationis nouitate mente conpungitur, lacrimis perfunditur et ei pre gaudio a fo. 81^r senectute et senio, 'sicut aquile iuuentus renouatur',[3] | et ipsis uelocior auibus, ut ita dicam, festinus aduolat, ut tanquam pennis eum magis uehi quam equis censeas. Citus aduenit; quod auribus insonuerat fidelibus oculis innotuit; 'uidit et gauisus est'.[4]

Accedens itaque ad singulare illud nostris temporibus et posteris mirabile monimentum, uidens mulieres, quasi circa Dominum lamentantes ipsum^a quasi in sepulcro iacentem, circumquaque assistentes, sicut in passione finem eius expectantes; de infimo cordis singultus eructans in uerba prorumpens ait:

viii. *Adoratio et oratio ipsius Thoui.*

'Domine pater, creator celi et terre, qui mundum ex nichilo creasti et omnia quecunque celi ambitu continentur, Dominus uniuersorum tu es. Domine, qui pro salute mundi corpus tuum et sanguinem patri in ara crucis hostiam sanctam Deoque placentem fo. 81^v exhibuisti, qui | spineam coronam pro salute fidelium capiti tuo applicari uoluisti, potatus absinthio et felle,[5] sitim nostre salutis

---

^a lamentantes et ipsum *H*

---

[1] The term *feodi* (fee) is used anachronistically of the time of Cnut.
[2] See above, pp. xvi–xviii.
[3] Ps. 102 (103): 5.
[4] John 8: 56.
[5] Cf. Matt. 27: 34; Lam. 3: 19.

7. The lord of the fee,[1] Tovi the Proud, is sent for.

Since nobody considered himself good enough to touch such a treasure with his hands, they decided to surround the place with tents because of the inclement weather and the need to keep careful watch. They resolved to choose devout persons, both men and women, to keep watch during the night in faithful service until the marvellous event was reported to the lord of their lands, Tovi the Proud, being the first man in all England after the king, a staller[2] and standard-bearer of the king, accustomed to advising the monarch.

He was at that time occupied in distant parts of England, involved in royal business, being second only to the king: his general responsibilities were greater than those held by other magnates in the land, and he was closest to the king in his counsels; he also assisted the king in important matters of the realm. When he heard, therefore, of so recent a cause for rejoicing, he was pricked in his conscience and overcome by tears, but because of his joy, instead of feeling the weakness of age, 'his youth was renewed like the eagle's':[3] he flew, so to speak, with all speed, more swiftly than the very birds, so that you would have thought he was being conveyed rather on wings than by horses. He soon arrived, and what he had heard with his ears he now observed with believing eyes: 'he saw and rejoiced'.[4]

Approaching the relic, a remarkable and marvellous memorial in our own time and for future ages, he saw the women standing all around weeping, as if they were around the Lord as He lay in the tomb, just as the women had waited for His end at His passion: with a groan that rose from the depth of his being Tovi poured out these words:

8. Tovi's adoration and prayer.

'O Lord and Father, creator of heaven and earth, who created out of nothing the world and all things contained within the circle of the heavens, you are lord of all. O Lord who, to save the world, sacrificed your body and blood to the Father on the altar of the cross, a holy victim, well-pleasing to God, who allowed the crown of thorns to be placed upon your head for the salvation of the faithful, who, by drinking the wormwood and the gall,[5] have

amaritudine potus illius dulcorasti, quique in illius potus consuma-
tione literam legis nouitate spiritus tui gentibus innouasti,[1] te laudo,
te adoro, te glorifico, tibi gratias ago[2] quod me dignatus es tantis
beneficiis participem fieri et terram nostram tue gratie beneficio
illustrari; exultatio mea, pax et gaudium cordis mei, illustratio spiritus mei, firmitas et compago menbrorum meorum, refocillatio
anime mee, spes et salus uite mee, tibi gloria in seculorum secula.'

ix. *Qualiter consilio optimatum decreuit Thoui paruam crucem ibidem
dimittere. Et uouit magnam crucem cum ceteris, Londiniis, Wintonie,
Cantuarie, Glastonie, Redingiis, et stetit plaustrum immobile.*

Quid cordis, quid animi, quid spiritus erat populis hec audientibus! Tremebat plebs omnis uelut expectans terribilis buccine
fo. 82ʳ sonitum inuitantis | ad iuditium. Nutabat prediues ille quo trans-
ferret condigne hoc mirabile sanctificium. Sedit autem menti eius,
communi optimatum consilio in uallis planitiem usque in atrium[3]
ecclesie hec sacrosancta perducere, ut de plano iuga boum hiis
applicata facilius possint distraere, quocumque uellet ea dominus
fundi transferre. Sicut Domino placuit ita factum est; sit nomen
eius benedictum in secula.

Fessus[a] itaque diuinis laboribus et internis gemitibus heros ille,
domini regis uexillarius, post sumptos cibos cum menbra dedisset
quieti, cepit instanter et deuotissime meditari quid operis, quidue
consilii in hiis condigne distribuendis expediat illi. Mane autem eo
surgente optimatumque stipato agmine, post celebrationem diui-
fo. 82ᵛ norum, communi omnium consilio decretum est | minorem
crucem in ecclesia ibi presenti dimittere, cetera circumferre quo
diuine uoluntati nouerint conplacere. Plaustro ea inserunt, cum
ornamentorum decora uarietate iungunt boues .xii. rubeos, iungunt et hiis totidem uaccas niueas,[4] boum custodes cum stimulis,
armamenta simul eis necessaria que non deficiant in uia si trans-
ferantur ad loca remota.

[a] fessis *CH*

---

[1] Cf. Rom. 7: 6.

[2] Cf. the *Gloria*: 'Laudamus te, adoramus te, glorificamus te, gratias agimus tibi.'

[3] The present church of St Catharine at Montacute claims to date from *c.* 1000 and is a few hundred yards from the steep, conical St Michael's hill.

[4] The description has all the trappings of religious symbolism: the number 12 (the 12 tribes of Israel, the 12 apostles) and the colours, 'red' of the blood of Christ, 'white' of the purity of the Virgin.

sweetened our thirst for our own salvation through the bitterness of that cup, and by so draining that cup have replaced the letter of the law with the new life of your Spirit for mankind,[1] I praise you, I worship you, I glorify you, I give thanks to you[2] that you have deemed me worthy of sharing in such blessings, and our land worthy of being honoured by the benefits of your grace: O source of my delight, O peace and joy of my heart, enlightener of my spirit, O strength and sustainer of my body, restorer of my soul, the hope and saviour of my life, glory be to you for ever and ever.'

9. *On the advice of his leading men Tovi decreed that the small cross should be left where it was. He promised the large cross with the other relics to London, Winchester, Canterbury, Glastonbury, and Reading. The wagon refused to move.*

How stirred the people were in heart, mind, and spirit when they heard these words! All the common folk trembled as though they were expecting the sound of the fearful trumpet calling them to judgement. Tovi, a man of great wealth, could not decide where it was most appropriate to convey this marvellous holy thing. With the common consent of the leading men he decided to take these holy things to the churchyard[3] on the floor of the valley so that the yokes of the oxen could more easily be fitted to these beasts on the level ground for them to convey the relics wherever the lord of the estate wished. So God's will was done, blessed be His name for ever!

The noble Tovi, standard bearer of our lord the king, exhausted by his holy toil and his inner emotion, lay down after supper to rest his limbs. However, he began immediately, with great devotion, to consider what he could best do or plan in order to distribute these holy things most appropriately. He rose early and after the celebration of divine service, surrounded by a band of leading men he decided, with the consent of all these men, to leave the smaller cross there in the local church, and take the other relics around to places where they knew it would please God. They put them in a wagon to which they harnessed twelve red oxen handsomely accoutred with a variety of trappings, and to these they yoked as many white cows;[4] there were herdsmen with goads, and they also took essential equipment so that they might not be without them on the way should things have to be conveyed to distant places.

Facta denique oratione a clero et omni populo, quod det Dominus spiritum consilii domino Toui ad destinanda presentia quo sue complaceat uoluntati, cum uoueret ea dominus Toui ubi tunc erat archiepiscopatus, Doroberni, Wintonie, Glastonie, Londonie, et diuersis episcopatuum sedibus et abbatiarum Anglie, stetit carrum quasi fixum nec poterat moueri tractu boum uel fo. 83ʳ impulsu hominum. Reminiscens | tandem cuiusdam domicilii sui, in quo plurimum conplacuit illi, scilicet Redinges, orat Christum profusis lacrimis ut bene placitum sit in oculis eius transferri ea illuc, tutamen[1] et ornamentum sibi et suis successoribus, et ipse totam daret uillam sancte crucis seruientibus cum omnibus eidem adiacentibus. Stetit plaustrum, trahitur, impellitur, iuga boum prioribus adibentur nec mouetur. Spectant attoniti qui affuere, certi hoc sine prouidentia non agi uoluntatis diuine.

x. *Qualiter tandem nominata uilla de Waltham, mouit se plaustrum et curatur multitudo infirmorum in itinere.*

Vota uotis addit ille heros magne celsitudinis, et uouendo a celsioribus ecclesiis ad inferiores descendens non est exauditus, quia reseruauit ea Deus alto consilio alteri loco quem digniorem censuit presentium benefitio.[a] Memor tandem pauperis tugurii fo. 83ᵛ quod edi|ficare ceperat in loco siluestri quod nunc Waltham dicitur, locus scilicet amenus, siluis uberrimis circumcinctus, fluuio piscium uberrimo qui Legia dicitur ornatus, amenitate pratorum fertilium decorus, Londoniis satis propinquus, Thamensi fluuio flumine predicto influente contiguus, decernit initiale benefitium, quod iam cepit, ampliori margine dilatare si uelit ea Deus ad hec loca transmittere. Mirabile dictu! fide mirabilius! cum insonuisset nomen Waltham ilico mouit se plaustrum, ita ut magis plaustrum boues inpellere quam ipsos boues plaustrum trahere censeres. Gaudio percelluntur corda fidelium et felici ducatu insequentes imaginem crucifixi, exultant successibus quos opera-fo. 84ʳ tus est Deus benefitio prestito | languentibus.

ᵃ *om. H*

---

[1] Saints and relics were regarded as protectors of their churches and patrons, particularly in times of trouble. See Geary, *Furta Sacra*, pp. 20–2; H. Fichtenau, 'Zum Reliquienwesen im früheren Mittelalter', *Mitteilungen des Instituts für Österreichische Geschichtsforschung*, lx (1952), 60–89.

Finally the clergy and all the people prayed that God would give the spirit of wisdom to Lord Tovi that he might send these present relics to wherever God willed. Tovi then promised them to Canterbury, the seat of the archbishop at that time, to Winchester, Glastonbury, and London, as well as to other places in England where there were seats of bishops or abbots. The cart stood still as if rooted there, and it could not be moved either by the pulling of the oxen or the pushing of the men. Remembering at last an abode of his of which he was very fond at Reading, he prayed to Christ with many tears that He be pleased to grant the removal of the relics to that place to be a protection[1] and an honour to Tovi and to his descendants: he would give the whole of his vill with all the land around it to those serving the holy cross. But the wagon stood still; it was pushed, it was pulled, yokes of oxen were added to the animals in front, but it did not move. Those who were there looked on in astonishment, convinced that this was not happening without the providence and will of God.

10. *At last the vill of Waltham was mentioned and the wagon moved off. A large number of sick people were healed on the journey.*

The high and noble Tovi continued with prayer after prayer. In naming places he moved from the more important churches to those of less importance, but he was not heard because God in His profound wisdom decreed those relics for another place which He deemed more worthy of the benefit of this gift. At last he remembered a lowly hut which he had begun to build in a woodland region which is now called Waltham, a pleasant place surrounded by luxuriant woods, provided with a river full of fish which is called the Lea; its picturesque, fertile meadows made it a delightful spot. It was quite close to London and near the River Thames of which the Lea is a tributary. His original estate which he had already begun he decided to extend within a wider boundary if God willed that the relics be transported to this place. Marvellous to say! more marvellous to believe! when he had mentioned the name of Waltham the wagon instantly moved, so that you would have thought that the cart was pushing the oxen rather than the oxen themselves pulling the cart. The hearts of the faithful were stirred with joy, and following the image of the crucified one behind their happy leaders, they rejoiced in the successful outcome which God had wrought and in the gift bestowed upon the weary.

Nam ut primi patres qui affuerunt filiis suis memorabile reli-
querunt, et nos successiue ab illis didicimus et firma fide tenemus,
a motione plaustri usque ad decensum in Waltham crucifixi, in-
finitis reparatio sanitatis ex diuersis languoribus restituta est. De
quibus .lxvi., qui se uouerunt usque ad consummationem uite
seruituros sancte cruci, in primis instituta est uilla Walthamensis:
nam antea nichil erat in loco nisi uile domicilium ad succurrendum
cum causa uenandi accederet illuc heros ille.[1] Habebat enim in
confinio illius loci predia multa: Enefelde, Edelmetun, Cetrehunt,
Mimmes et baroniam[2] quam nunc habet comes Willelmus de
Mandeuile[3] et multo hiis ampliora sed hunc locum selegerat[a]
fo. 84[v] propter habundantiam ferarum | siluestrium, summe quietis.[b]
Hanc uillam fundasse et hiis .lxvi. uiris primo instituisse accepimus a patribus nostris, deinde successiue creuit usque ad presentia tempora sicut uidere possunt qui nunc extant.

xi. *Qualiter exiuit sanguis de brachio dextro quando laminam clauo firmare
uoluerunt.*

Ab huius crucis inuentione transeundum est ad ipsius exalta-
tionem, quia semel humiliatus est[c] Deus et homo usque ad infima
mundi, postea ascendit ad summa fastigia celi ubi coeternus patri
residet ad dexteram ipsius, regnans et inperans, iudicans uiuos et
mortuos[4] et seculum per ignem.[5] Audiuimus autem huic exalta-
tioni a nobili uiro Toui excitos ex diuersis regni partibus multos
heroum euocari, ut huic interessent solempnitati, ut mererentur
participes exaltationis fieri quibus non datum est inuentioni.
fo. 85[r] Multiplici igitur | opere fabrili gemmarum, auri, et argenti pre-
munierat se gloriosus heros ille Toui quo redimere posset corpus
crucifixi, set a seculis inauditum contigit memorabile factum, nam

---

[a] se elegerat *CH*   [b] quieti *CH*   [c] *om. C*

---

[1] See above, p. xv.
[2] *Baroniam* is here used with its 12th-cent. meaning, as a feudal honour held of the
king.
[3] William the Conqueror gave some of Tovi's former estates to Geoffrey de Mandeville (see above, p. xxvii), and they passed after some vicissitudes to his descendants
(C. Warren Hollister, 'The misfortunes of the Mandevilles', *Monarchy, Magnates and
Institutions in the Anglo-Norman World* (London and Ronceverte, 1986), pp. 117–27).
William de Mandeville, earl of Essex, died in 1189; his death gives a *terminus ante quem*
for the writing of the Chronicle.

Our forefathers who witnessed it have left this account to their children, and we who in our turn have learned it from them believe it with all our hearts, that from the moment the wagon began to move right up to the time the cross came down into Waltham, countless numbers of people who were suffering from all sorts of diseases were restored to health. Of these, sixty-six dedicated themselves to the service of the holy cross to the end of their lives, and the vill of Waltham was first founded by them. Before this there was nothing in this place but a poor dwelling intended to provide lodgings for the noble Tovi when he came here to hunt.[1] He possessed many estates in the neighbourhood of that place: these were Enfield, Edmonton, Cheshunt, Mimms, and the barony[2] which Earl William de Mandeville[3] now possesses. In fact he owned much larger estates than these, but he had selected this place because of the large number of woodland beasts here, and because of its great peacefulness. We have learned from our forefathers that he founded this vill and first established it with these sixty-six men. Then it grew in course of time to what it is today, as those who are now alive can see.

11. *Blood oozed from the right arm when they attempted to nail a plate to it.*

We must now pass on from our account of the discovery of the cross to its exaltation, for He who once humbled Himself and descended to the very depths of the earth as God and man afterwards ascended to the highest vaults of heaven where, co-eternal with the Father, He sits at His right hand reigning in power, judging the living and the dead[4] and the present world by fire.[5] We have heard it said that the noble Tovi sent to men of high position in different parts of the realm, and invited them to attend this ceremony, so that those who had not been granted the privilege of witnessing the discovery might have the honour of participating in the exaltation.

The high and noble Tovi now secured the skills of many craftsmen in precious stones, gold, and silver with which he could adorn the body of the crucified Christ. It was then that an amazing event occurred unheard of ever before, for in attaching the adornment

---

[4] Cf. 2 Tim. 4: 1.
[5] Cf. 1 Cor. 3: 13.

et in ornatu apponendo, dum primo clauo[1] firmare uellent in brachio dextro laminam ad hoc ductilem, exiuit sanguis ex silice[2] cernentibus cunctis qui aderant, et mirantibus Dei uirtutem et ineffabilem potentiam, qui de silice[a] aquas productiores elicit, qui grana frumenti et expressionem botri transformat in corpus suum et sanguinem, qui de arboribus et fructicibus fructus producit, et de silicibus ignem; set satis admiratione dignum inueniet qui facta eius mirabilia mirari contendit.

Sanguinem hunc, de silice elicitum Dei nutu, et in lintheamine corporali susceptum, nos uidere et in capsa argentea repositum[5] |
fo. 85[v] miseratione diuina meruimus, quos a teneris annis educauit ecclesia Walthamiensis .liii. annis,[3] et in gremio suo literalibus instruxit disciplinis.[b4] Me miserum quod datum est uidere in hac uita quod separer ab uberibus matris mee!

xii. *Adoratio Thoui et donaria eius, scilicet Waltham, Hicche, Luketune etc, cum ense quo erat accinctus miles.*

Admiratione igitur tanti miraculi stupefactus Toui, indignum se censens[c] uisione tali, publicano similis qui nec oculos audebat ad celos leuare,[6] reminiscens etiam quod si iniquitates nostre contenderint contra nos et obseruauerit eas Dominus,[7] non iustificabitur in conspectu eius omnis uiuens homo, nec infans cuius est uita unius diei super terram,[8] deposito insigni quo induebatur habitu et sacco uestitus, more pueri balbutientis, cepit manibus et genibus
fo. 86[r] reptare ad locum | ubi memorabilis iacebat ymago crucifixi, ad quam uoce lugubri, corde contrito et humiliato non sine multa lacrimarum effusione, ita exorsus est: 'Adoro te Christe pendentem in ligno pro salute fidelium, quod michi representat presens istud exemplar tue passionis; adoro te, Domine, infernum uisitantem et in sanctis

[a] salice *H*   [b] discipulis *H*   [c] senciens *H*

---

[1] Reference is made in the work of the medieval metalworker Theophilus to the practice of fastening thin sheets of gold and silver to objects by means of studs: 'si aurum uel argentum laminis attenuatum atque clauis alicubi confixum' (Theophilus, *The Various Arts: De Diuersis Artibus*, ed. and trans. C. R. Dodwell (OMT, 1986), p. 142).

[2] In very different circumstances the image on the cross at Glastonbury was said by William of Malmesbury to bleed when struck by an arrow during the disturbances in the church in 1083 (William of Malmesbury, *De Antiquitate Glastonie Ecclesie*, ed. John Scott (Woodbridge, 1981), pp. 158–9).

[3] The college was dissolved in 1177; this dates the entry of the author to *c.* 1124.

[4] See above, pp. xxx–xxxi.

they were attempting to put in the first stud[1] to secure to the right arm the plating which had been hammered out for this purpose, when blood oozed from the rock.[2] All who were present saw this, and marvelled at the goodness and the unspeakable power of God, who draws streams of water from rock, who changes the grain of corn and the juice of the grape into his own body and blood, who makes trees and bushes yield fruit and the flint produce fire. The man who strives to marvel at God's wonderful deeds will find this event most worthy of his admiration.

Those of us whom the church at Waltham has nurtured over a period of fifty-three years[3] and lovingly instructed in the discipline of letters[4] were honoured by God's mercy to see this blood, which had been drawn from the stone by the will of God and caught in the linen of a corporal cloth,[5] and preserved in a silver casket. Alas, that I should have lived to see myself separated from the bosom of my mother church!

12. *Tovi's worship and gifts; namely, Waltham, Hitchin, Loughton, etc. and the sword with which he had been girded as a knight.*

Tovi was therefore struck with amazement at such a miracle, considering himself unworthy of seeing such a thing, like the publican who did not dare to raise his eyes to heaven,[6] remembering also that if our sins cry out against us and the Lord marks them[7] no man living, nor child who has lived but one day on earth, shall be justified in his sight.[8] So he laid aside the fine cloak which he was wearing and, clothed in sackcloth, he began to crawl on hands and knees like a prattling infant to the place where the remarkable crucifix lay. There with mournful voice and humble, contrite heart he began with copious tears to utter these words: 'I worship you, O Christ, hanging there on the tree for the salvation of the faithful, for this represents for me a present likeness of your passion. I worship you, O Lord, for visiting Hell and leading the souls of the holy

---

[5] Since the blood was considered as Christ's blood it was treasured as a relic; similarly, when the consecrated wine was spilt on the carpet during a papal Mass at Reims in 1148, the piece of carpet was cut out and placed among the relics in the cathedral church (John of Salisbury, *Historia Pontificalis*, ed. Marjorie Chibnall (OMT, 1986), p. 11).

[6] Luke 18: 13.

[7] Cf. Ps. 129 (130): 3.

[8] Cf. Ps. 142 (143): 2.

animabus inferos triumphantem;[1] adoro te a mortuis resurgentem, morte tua mortem fidelium consummantem; adoro te in celum ascendentem ad consessum patris et abinde spiritum tuum in corda discipulorum et eorum pure sequatium mittentem; tibi laus, tibi gloria, honor perpes et inperium sit in secula seculorum. Me tibi deuotum constituo, quecumque mancipia, quocumque modo adquisita, libera tibi imperpetuum trado, uillam presentem |

fo. 86ᵛ scilicet Waltham,[2] et Chenleuedene, Hicche,[a] et Lamhee, Lukentune et Alwaretone,[3] ad sustentamentum tibi seruituris in perpetuum do', et hiis dictis ensem quo[b] primo fuerat accinctus miles factus circumcinxit ymagini, amodo militaturus illi; et applicato eo super crucem ligneam laminis argenteis fecit inuolui, quia se clauis nullo modo permisit infigi.

xiii. *Qualiter Glitha uxor Thoui dedit coronam auream, circulum, et suppeditaneum cum lapide.*

Vxor autem eius, Glitha nomine, filia Osegodi Scalp,[4] uiri uenerabilis et ditissimi, mulier religiosa et sanctis exercitiis dedita, mirifico ex proprio sumptu artifitio formatam capiti illius circumdedit coronam ex auro obrizo et lapidibus preciosissimis obstructam, ob memoriam spinee corone, cuius punctiones et obprobria passus est pro nostra salute. Circulum quoque insignem ex auro

fo. 87ʳ purissimo quali[c] tunc | temporis utebantur nobilissime matrone circumcinxit eius femori, mirifico lapidum ornatu constructum, et ex eodem auro subpedaneum[5] ex monilibus et armillis suis conpactum, in quo et lapidem infigi precepit, qui furua nocte obductis luminaribus radios emittit ut circumstantibus[6] possit lumen subclarum ad notitiam discernendarum rerum[d] prebere.

Hunc centum marcis[8] emere et Wintoniam transferre cupiuit Henricus, episcopus illius ecclesie, tunc quidem decanus noster,[7]

[a] Hyche *H*   [b] cum *H*   [c] quale *H*   [d] iter *H*

[1] The 'descent of Christ into Hell' was based on a number of Biblical passages, such as 1 Peter 3: 18–20; Eph. 4: 9, and found its way into the Apostles' Creed. The Harrowing of Hell was a popular theme in medieval literature and art.
[2] Although the original extent of the canons' holding in Waltham (Essex) where the church was built is uncertain, this is clearly the Waltham implied here, and not West Waltham (Berks.), as Stubbs thought.
[3] See above, pp. xxiii–xxiv.   [4] See above, pp. xvi–xvii.
[5] The suppedaneum was the support for the feet of Christ.
[6] Later the duties of the *custos ecclesie* would have included taking care of treasures in the church; possibly the sacristan would have had this duty in Tovi's church.
[7] Henry of Blois, bishop of Winchester, was a notorious collector of works of art and

dead in triumph;[1] I worship you for rising from the dead and by your death putting an end to death for the faithful; I worship you for ascending into Heaven to sit beside the Father, and for sending from there your Holy Spirit into the hearts of the disciples and those who follow you with a pure heart. To you be praise, to you be glory, never-ending honour and power for ever and ever. I dedicate myself to you, and freely surrender for ever my possessions, however obtained, and give you for ever this vill of Waltham,[2] and *Chenlevedene*, Hitchin, Lambeth, Loughton, and Alderton[3] to sustain those who will serve you.' With these words he fastened around the figure of Christ the sword with which he had been girded when he was first made a knight, intending henceforth to fight only for Him; and when he had fastened it to the wooden cross he had the cross overlaid with silver plating, though he would in no wise allow this to be fastened with studs.

13. *Tovi's wife Gytha gave a golden crown and belt, and a suppedaneum fitted with a stone.*

Tovi's wife, named Gytha, daughter of Osgod Clapa,[4] a highly respected and wealthy man, being a devout woman dedicated to holy works, placed upon the head of Christ a crown of marvellous workmanship purchased at her own expense. It was of pure gold and embossed with precious stones as a memorial of the crown of thorns, whose pains and dishonour Christ suffered for our salvation. She also put around His loins a remarkable girdle of purest gold, of the kind which women of the highest rank wore in those days, and it was adorned with a marvellous decoration of gemstones. Then she had a suppedaneum[5] made of the same gold obtained from her own necklaces and bracelets, and she gave instructions for a gemstone to be set in it which glowed when the night was dark and the lamps had been put out, so that it could provide a dim light for those on watch,[6] to illuminate the things they needed to see.

Henry, bishop of Winchester, at the time when he was also our dean[7] wanted to purchase this stone for one hundred marks[8]

treasures for his church; he secured for a time, amongst other acquisitions, the hand of St James which had been given to Reading (see K. J. Leyser, 'Frederick Barbarossa, Henry II and the Hand of St James', *Medieval Germany and its Neighbours 900–1250* (London, 1982), pp. 215–40, at 225–31). Henry of Blois appears in only one Waltham charter (July 1141 × September 1143) in his capacity as dean of Waltham (Ransford, *Waltham Charters*, no. 22); he was replaced by another dean also called Henry not later than 1146 or 1147 (ibid., no. 23).

[8] The value of the mark of silver in the 12th cent. was 13s. 4d. (66.6 new pence).

set in ueritate que Deus est, nec illud nec minimam ornamentorum portionem, permisimus ab ecclesia transferri, licet modo peccatis nostris exigentibus, inter infimos regni clericos dampnationi regio edicto simus deputati.¹ Nouit tamen Dominus qui sunt eius, nouit grana, nouit paleas, set cum triturabitur | area reponentur grana in apothecam*a* uentilatis paleis,² reponetur uinum eiectis uinatiis, horreis mandabuntur legumina eiectis siliquis.

fo. 87ᵛ

xiiii. *Defuncto Thoui successit filius eius Adelstanus qui amisit Waltham, quam adeptus est comes Haraldus per sanctum Eadwardum.*

Eleuata igitur cruce solempni et cunctis circa eam rite dispositis, presbiteros duos instituit cum reliquis clericis Deo ministraturos in ecclesia, quibus et ipse deuotione comes effectus cum uxore nobili non destitit toto tempore uite sue eam auro et argento, ornamentis quoque preciosis indesinenter ornare.

Tandem consumatus in breui expleuerat tempora multa, cui successit filius eius Adelstanus, pater Esegari qui stallere*b* inuentus est in Anglie*c* conquisitione a Normannis,³ cuius hereditatem postea dedit conquisitor terre, rex Willelmus, Galfrido de Mandeuile, proauo presentis comitis Willelmi.⁴ Successit quidem Adelstanus patri suo | Toui non in totam quidem*d* possessionem quam possederat pater, set in eam tantum que pertinebat ad stallariam,⁵ quam nunc habet comes Willelmus. Amplas enim sibi conquisierat possessiones Toui preter hereditatem propriam,⁶ tum indita ei sapientia qua precipuus erat inter primos terre, tum quia in consiliis domini regis primus prodesse poterat uel obesse quibus uolebat, tum quia domini regis gratiam qui multa ei de proprio suo contulerat habere meruit.

fo. 88ʳ

Set degenerans a patris astutia et sapientia filius multa ex hiis perdidit, et inter cetera Waltham quam defuncto Cnuto et Hardecnuto

---

a apotecham *C*   *b* stalre *C*   *c* *lacuna after* Angli- *C*   *d* quidam *H*

---

¹ See above, p. xxviii. The author is referring to the canons' loss of status after the dissolution of the college; they were allowed to keep their prebends for life if they wished.
² Cf. Luke 3: 17.
³ See above, p. xvii.
⁴ See above, p. 18 n. 2.
⁵ See above, p. xvii. It is not clear from this very general statement whether all the land attached to Tovi's stallership was included in the estates given to Geoffrey de Mandeville.
⁶ See above, p. xvii.

and to carry it off to Winchester, but it is God's truth that we did not allow that stone or the smallest portion of these adornments to be transferred from the church, though as punishment for our sins we have now been condemned by royal edict to be amongst the lowest of the clergy of the realm.[1] Yet the Lord knows those who are His, He knows the wheat, He knows what is chaff, and when His threshing-floor is cleaned the wheat will be placed in the storehouse and the chaff winnowed out,[2] the wine will be bottled and the grapestones and skin thrown away, the legumes will be placed safely in the storehouses and the pods rejected.

14. *On his death Tovi was succeeded by his son Athelstan who lost Waltham, but Earl Harold gained it through St Edward.*

When the cross had been solemnly elevated and everything arranged duly around it, Tovi appointed two priests with other clerks to serve God in the church. He himself, having become a fellow-worker with them by his devotion, did not cease with his noble wife to adorn the church throughout the whole of his life with gold and silver, and with precious ornaments as well.

By the end of his life he had accomplished the work of many generations in a short period. He was succeeded by his son Athelstan, father of Asgar who was a staller at the time of the Norman conquest of England,[3] and whose inheritance the conqueror of the land, King William, later gave to Geoffrey de Mandeville, great-grandfather of the present Earl William.[4] Athelstan, in fact, did not inherit from his father the whole of the property possessed by Tovi, but only that which related to his stallership,[5] the land which is now held by Earl William. Tovi had acquired for himself large possessions apart from the land he had inherited,[6] first because of the wisdom with which he was endowed that gave him a special place among the leading men in the land, then because, as first man in the councils of his lord the king, he was able to benefit or harm anyone he wished, thirdly because he earned the gratitude of his lord the king who conferred upon him many of his own possessions.

However, his son lacked his father's astuteness and wisdom, and lost many of these possessions, amongst others Waltham which, after the death of Cnut and his son Harthacnut, King Edward

eius filio cum imperaret Anglis et regni regimen suscepisset, beate memorie rex Edwardus dedit comiti Haraldo,[1] comitis Godwini filio, fratri etiam beate memorie Edithe regine, qui armis strenuus, fo. 88ᵛ procero corpore et | inestimabili strenuitate, forma etiam pulcritudinis precellens cunctis primatibus terre, regis manus dextera, et sapientia preditus, et artium omnium que decent militem gnarus, se uirum agebat preclarum per omnia. Nec derogare credimus ipsius excellentie quod predecessoris sui, scilicet Toui, imitator effectus in sancte crucis ueneratione, collata ei benefitia firma et illibata manere constituerit, presertim cum sepe uiderimus predecessorum opera, successoribus inuisa, debilem statum obtinuisse.

Nam toto tempore uite ipsius, quasi uterinus filius ecclesie factus, opibus eam ditare, donariis augere, auro, argento, et gemmis prefulgentem exhibere sategit, presertim reliquiarum[2] multiplicitate quatenus poterat prece uel precio, in diuersis terrarum partibus non segnis conquisitor fuit. Gratiam enim fo. 89ʳ domini regis et omnium prediuitum terre, tam ec|clesiasticorum quam laicorum, ita singularem adquisierat, tumᵃ gratia regine sororis sue et patris eorum qui successerat Toui in regimine totius Anglie post regem consiliis,[3] et astutia et legum terre peritia, tum quia se talem gerebat quod non solum Angli, uerum etiam Normanni et Gallici ipsius inuidebant pulcritudini et prudentie, militie et sagacitati; quem indigene pre ceteris postulabant et ardenter sitiebant post sanctum regem Edwardum, ipsius morum et uite heredem. Quod quidem diuina miserationeᵇ processu temporis uidere meruerunt qui tunc presentes fuerunt.

xv. *Haraldus adauxit possessiones; distinxit .xii. prebendas; fecit decanum; uictualia ordinauit.*

Duobus igitur predictis clericis quos instituerat Toui le Prude in ecclesia Walthamensi, uir ille strenuus comes Haraldus .xi.ᶜ[4] sociauit

---

ᵃ cum *H*   ᵇ miseratione diuina *H*   ᶜ xi *H*; xi *later addition in C*

---

[1] This is confirmed by *DB*, i. 15b.

[2] A list of the relics said to have been brought to Waltham by Harold is preserved in BL Harley MS 3776, fos. 31–5, which has been critically edited by Nicholas Rogers, 'Waltham relic-list'.

[3] The author clearly exaggerated Tovi's importance; Earl Godwine was of higher rank and much greater wealth and importance (see Fleming, *Kings and Lords*, *passim*, esp. pp. 53–69). The date of Tovi's death is uncertain; see above, p. xix.

[4] See above, cap. 14, where Tovi is said to have appointed 'two priests with other

of blessed memory gave, after his succession to the throne and while he was ruling the English, to Earl Harold,[1] son of Earl Godwine, and brother of Queen Edith of blessed memory. Harold was a fine soldier, tall of stature, incredibly strong, more handsome than all the leading men in the land, and the king's right-hand man. He was endowed with wisdom, skilled in all the military arts which became a knight, and showed himself to be in all respects a man of distinction. We do not believe it detracts from this man's excellence that he imitated the devotion of his predecessor Tovi to the holy cross, and was determined that the benefits bestowed upon it should remain sure and undiminished, especially as we have often seen that the works of predecessors which are disliked by those who succeed them have suffered at their hands.

Throughout his whole life, like a true son of the Church, he occupied himself in making her rich in resources, heaping gifts upon her, and making her gleam with gold, silver and precious stones. He was particularly active in procuring as large a number of relics as he could from different parts of the world, either by request or by purchase.[2] In this way he had gained the singular favour of his lord the king and of all wealthy men in the land, both churchmen and laity; secondly, he won the favour of his sister the queen and of their father, who had succeeded Tovi in the control of all England,[3] being next to the king in his counsels, having astuteness and knowledge of the laws of the land; thirdly, he so behaved that not only the English, but also the Normans and the French, envied his handsome figure, his prudence, his knightly prowess, and his wisdom. His own countrymen chose him in preference to all others, and they fervently desired him as king after the saintly King Edward, and as the heir to his holy life. Those who were then living were privileged in due course by God's mercy to see this happen.

15. *Harold increased its possessions, established twelve prebends, appointed a dean, and arranged for provisions.*

Earl Harold, who was a man of great energy, accordingly added another eleven[4] men to the previously mentioned clerks whom

clerks'. The original figure (x) in MS *C* would imply a total of twelve including the dean; the *Vita Haroldi* (pp. 23, 123) also gave the number as twelve, probably copying the original *C* version of the Chronicle.

alios uiros prudentes, literatos, selectos[a] a communibus, inter precipuos | terre diligenter exquisitos, inter quos Theothonicum quendam, diuino munere et inexperato sibi collatum, magistrum Atdelardum, Leodicensem genere, Tragectensem[b] studii disciplina,[1] adhibuit, quatinus leges, instituta, et consuetudines, tam in ecclesiasticis quam in secularibus, ecclesiarum in quibus educatus fuerat, in ecclesia Walthamensi constitueret; quoniam multorum relatione didicerat ordinatissima distinctione regi Theutonicorum ecclesias ut siquid dignum ultione uel correptione inter clericos oriretur, a decano ecclesie siue ab ipso magistro Athelardo, excessus acri uerbo, enormitates flagello, inmania etiam peccata ipsius prebende priuatione, multarentur. Quod et predecessorum nostrorum temporibus inoleuisse et usque ad tempora pueritie nostre perdurasse non ambigimus.

Hiis autem duodecim clericis perhibetur comes | ille Wlwinum decanum prefecisse, uirum religiosum, moribus illustrem, doctrina literali uenustum, speciali castitatis prerogatiua fulgentem,[2] qui cum magistro Adelardo ecclesie statum ita distinctum ordinauerunt. Vnicuique assignata est portio sua in prebendam, ut, deductis expensis que fratrum uictualibus exibere debebant, quod residuum erat in proprios usus loco prebende cederet. Sunt autem hee portiones quas in usus ecclesie assignauit comes Haroldus, una cum Toui, ad uictualia canonicorum per omnes anni septimanas, ut unusquisque firmas debitas de maneriis suis temporibus solueret.[3] Decanus pro Walda et Passefelda et Alrichesa .xix. ebdomadarum firmas; prebenda de Netleswelle[c] .vii. firmas et .ii. dies; Alwaretona .iiii. septimanas et .ii. dies;[d] Vpmenstre .ii. septi|manas et .ii. dies; Wodeford .ii. septimanas; Luketune unam septimanam et unum diem; Tipendene .ii. septimanas; Brichendone .ii. septimanas. Decano cessit pre ceteris West Waltham ut

fo. 89ᵛ

fo. 90ʳ

fo. 90ᵛ

---

[a] set electos *H*; se electos *later emendation in C*   [b] Tragrettensem *H*
[c] Nettliswelle *H*   [d] Alwaretona .iiii. septimanas et .ii. dies *om. H*

---

[1] See above, pp. xxi–xxii, xxx, xlvii.
[2] This implies that Wulwin, unlike Master Adelard, was not married.
[3] The system of 'food farms' to provide a regular supply of food throughout the year is known to have existed in many ecclesiastical institutions in the 11th and early 12th cents. Lennard, *Rural England*, pp. 130–2, provides early evidence for Bury St Edmunds, and evidence of slightly more uncertain date for the abbeys of Ramsey, St Albans, Ely, Abingdon, and the cathedrals of Canterbury, Rochester, and Worcester. For the 12th-cent. arrangements at St Pauls, London, see Christopher Brooke and Gillian Keir, *London 800–1216: The Shaping of a City* (London, 1978), pp. 352–3. The

Tovi the Proud had appointed in the church at Waltham. These new men were wise and educated, selected by the community and chosen with care from among the best men in the land. Amongst these was a certain German brought to his attention by God's unhoped-for goodness. This was Master Adelard, a native of Liège who had been a student at Utrecht.[1] He admitted him so that he could establish in the church at Waltham the rules, ordinances, and customs, both ecclesiastical and secular, of the churches in which he himself had been educated. Harold had discovered from the reports of many people that German churches were controlled by a very carefully regulated discipline. So, if anything deserving punishment or reproof were to occur among the clerks, they would be punished by the dean of the church or by Master Adelard himself: for minor sins they would receive a sharp reprimand, for more serious transgressions they would be punished by flogging, and for outrageous behaviour they would be deprived of the prebend itself. There is no doubt in my mind that such behaviour had increased in the times of my predecessors and had continued right up to the time of my childhood.

The earl is said to have appointed Wulwin over these twelve clerks as their dean, a devout man of high moral character, and distinguished for learning, a shining example of perfect chastity.[2] With Master Adelard he established the distinctive constitution of this church. To each clerk was assigned his own portion for his prebend so that, after necessary expenses had been deducted to pay for the brethren's food and drink, what was left counted as an allowance for their personal use. Along with the provisions made by Tovi the following are the portions which Earl Harold assigned for use of the church to provide food and drink for the canons every week of the year so that each of the canons could pay the farms due from his manors for specified periods.[3] The dean, from his estates at South Weald, Paslow, and Arlesey, was to be responsible for the farms of nineteen weeks; the prebend of Netteswell, for seven weeks and two days; Alderton, for four weeks and two days; Upminster, for two weeks and two days; Woodford, for two weeks; Loughton, for one week and one day; Debden, for two weeks; Brickendon, for two weeks. He granted West Waltham to the dean

Waltham Chronicle is interesting evidence of a system that almost certainly went back into the 11th-cent., though the chronicler may have described customs as they had developed when he first knew them in the 1120s. See above, p. xxiv.

aliis in eo precelleret qui primatum et regimen ceterorum habebat, in uictualibus etiam aliquantisper magis auctus quia pluribus habebat benefacere quam simplex canonicus.[1]

Erat enim distincta sic uniuscuiusque portio in septimana a sabbato usque ad sabbatum, cotidie .ii. panes albissimi, tercius minus albus, hii tres certe sufficientes discrete .vi. hominibus in prandio uno. Sex bolle ceruisie apte sufficientes in cena una .x. hominibus; cotidie .vi. fercula, unumquodque diuersi generis in profestis diebus. In festis uero diebus prime dignitatis tres pitantie unicuique, in festis secunde dignitatis due, in festis tertie dignitatis una. Erant fo. 91ʳ autem tales pitantie unicuique | canonico: a festo Sancti Michaelis usque ad caput ieiunii aut .xii. merule aut .ii. agausee aut .ii. perdices aut unus phasianus, reliquis temporibus aut auce aut galline. In precipuis festiuitatibus anni, Natali, festo Paschali, et Pentecosten et duobus festis Sancte Crucis, unicuique uinum et medo.[2] Collati sunt etiam in aucmentum predictorum unicuique canonico redditus .xl. solidi ad uestimentorum suppletionem, quod anglice Scruland uocatur; et in eadem uilla Waltham, unicuique .xv. acre assignate que Northlandeᵃ uocantur[3] ut e uicino sibi gaudeant commodi aliquid habere, quoniam ceteri redditus, in partibus distincti remotioribus, non eis proueniebant de facili. Preterea unicuique canonico .xl. solidi de obuentionibus altaris et decimationum[4] fo. 91ᵛ nomine commune. Multa etiam et | alia que enumerata tedium auditoribus generarent. Sed transeundum est ad magis necessaria.

xvi. *Que uasa, que ornamenta, dedit Haroldus; et dedicari fecit ecclesiam.*

Cum autem hiis uir ille uenerabilis ecclesiam ditasset beneficiis, gaudens prerogatiuo sibi collatum munere, quod non esset secunda huic in regno ecclesia, in tam decenti amministratione

ᵃ Northhande *H*

---

[1] See above, p. xxiv.

[2] The allowances would have been sufficient to enable the canons to provide alms for one or more needy persons; by the 12th cent. they were probably being used to support families also. It is interesting to note that wild birds were included in the pittances only from Michaelmas to February, so anticipating the more recent game laws which protect the nesting season.

[3] According to the 1177 charter of Henry II (Ransford, *Waltham Charters*, no. 26) the 'shroudlands' were in Loughton and Nazeing, and there was also 'shoeland' in Walter Hall. 'Northland' was described in Edward the Confessor's charter as the ancient endowment of the church of Waltham.

rather than to the others so that he might thereby distinguish him from them as the head and ruler of the rest of them; to some extent he received a greater allowance of food and drink also, because he had to care for more people than had the ordinary canon.[1]

Each canon's portion was divided up each week as follows: from Saturday to Saturday, each day two loaves of the purest white bread, a third loaf not so white, these three loaves when divided carefully being certainly sufficient for six persons at one meal. Six bowls of ale were quite sufficient for ten persons at one meal. Every ordinary day there were six dishes of food, each one of a different kind, but on feast days of primary importance each man had three pittances of food, two on feast days of secondary importance, and one on feast days of third rank of importance. There were the following additional allowances for each of the canons: from Michaelmas to the beginning of Lent a choice of twelve black-birds, two plovers, two partridges, or one pheasant. For the rest of the year they could have either geese or chickens. At the main festivals of the year, namely Christmas, Easter, Pentecost, and the two feast days of the Holy Cross, each canon was allowed wine and mead.[2] In addition to these allowances, payments of forty shillings were made to each canon for the provision of clothes. This is called 'Shroudland payment' in English; and in the same vill of Waltham fifteen acres, called 'Northland', were assigned to each of them,[3] so that they could enjoy having some benefit from their neighbour-hood, since the revenue from other lands which were more distant was not so readily available to them. Furthermore a sum of forty shillings by way of commons was granted to each canon from altar offerings and tithes.[4] There were many other allowances also which would be tedious to hear if recounted. I must now pass on to more essential matters.

16. *The vessels and adornments which Harold gave, and his dedication of the church.*

When the beloved Harold had enriched the church with such endowments, rejoicing that he had been able to confer upon it such remarkable prosperity that there was no church in the kingdom which approached Waltham in its fine performance of

[4] Gifts of tithes to religious houses are analysed and fully discussed by Giles Constable, *Monastic Tithes from their Origins to the Twelfth Century* (Cambridge, 1964).

ecclesiasticorum officiorum, uel honesta fratrum conuersatione, cepit eam interius multis decorare muneribus. Venusto enim admodum opere a fundamentis[1] constructam ecclesiam, laminis ereis, auro undique superducto, capita columpnarum et bases flexurasque arcuum ornare fecit mira distinctione artificis;[2] .xii. etiam imagines apostolorum opere fusili, que deportarent altare aureum anterius; leones etiam eiusdem operis qui supportarent

fo. 92[r] altare posterius; ipsum etiam altare | ex auro mero compositum quadratum in medio sui habens modicum lapidem marmoreum in ecclesie ornamentum construxit.

Ministerio etiam altaris uasa necessaria, diebus precipuis aurea, profestis argentea, sufficienti copiositate inuenit. Quatuor etiam capsas aureas, .ix. argenteas, candelabra aurea et argentea, turribula, urceos et pelues, cruces tres aureas, .vi. argenteas; textus aureos tres magnos, .v. argenteos deauratos. Hec omnia miro fabrorum artificio exculta predictis adiecit. Vestimentorum etiam habundantiam, simplicium scilicet et compositorum auro textorum, in cappis et casulis, dalmaticis et tunicis, et ceteris, redimitis auro et margaritis, multam contulit ecclesie ita ut unius aurum casule, que uocabatur 'Dominus dixit ad me',[3] appen-

fo. 92[v] deretur | .xxvi. marcarum auri in deauratione.

Quam cum construxisset ecclesiam, miro tabulatu et latomorum studio diligenti fabricatam, dedicationi eius instanter inuigilans, ipsum regem sancte memorie Edwardum inuitauit ad nuptias Christi et ecclesie illius reginam sororem[a] suam et primos totius Anglie: Ginsi, primo archipresulem Eboracensem, quia tunc uacabat sedes Cantuarie,[4] reliquos etiam episcopos utrarumque sedium quos iuuat ad presens, sicut didicimus a predecessoribus, enumerare, set sedium eorum discretionem non mente tenemus: Ailnotus, Heremanus, Leowricus, et Willelmus, Ailmarus,[b] Lefwinus, Wlwinus, et Ailwinus, Ailricus, Walterus, et Giso Cirecestrensis[c] episcopus.[5] Abbates etiam quorum hic nomina

---

   [a] reginam etiam sororem *H*   [b] Almarcus *H*   [c] Cirescestrensis *H*

---

  [1] The statement that a church had been built *a fundamentis* implied a thorough rebuilding, but not that it had been built on a new site.

  [2] Stubbs suggested (p. 17 n. 67) that this might be a description of a *ciborium* rather than of the church itself. See above, p. xxvii.

  [3] A reference to Ps. 2: 7, 'Dominus dixit ad me: Filius meus es tu; ego hodie genui te', which was sung in the first Mass on Christmas Day. Biblical scenes were embroidered in gold on some Anglo-Saxon vestments, and as Dodwell has pointed out, there can be little doubt that the subject depicted on this chasuble was the nativity of Christ. The

ecclesiastical offices, or in the honourable behaviour of the brethren, he began to adorn the inside of the church with many beautiful
gifts. He employed the finest workmanship in the building of the
church from its very foundations,[1] using bronze plate and gold
inlay everywhere; he had the capitals of the columns, the bases,
and the twists of the arches adorned with a marvellous quality of
workmanship.[2] Twelve statues of the apostles were also cast to
support the front of the golden altar; lions were similarly cast to
support the rear of the altar. To adorn the church he had the altar
itself made rectangular and of pure gold, with a small marble stone
in its centre.

He provided in sufficient quantity the vessels necessary for
service of the altar, golden for special days, silver for ordinary days.
In addition there were four golden, and nine silver, reliquaries,
candlesticks of gold and silver, censers, ewers and basins, three
golden, and six silver crosses; there were three large golden gospel
books, and five of silver-gilt. All these things, the work of
wonderfully skilled craftsmen, he added to the items already
mentioned. In addition he provided the church with a large quantity of vestments, some made of unembroidered cloth and others
woven with gold thread: there were copes, chasubles, dalmatics,
tunics and other garments ornamented with gold and pearls;
indeed, the gold of one chasuble, which was called 'The Lord
Spake Unto Me',[3] was adorned with twenty-six marks of gold in
the gilding.

When he had built the church, and had it constructed of the
finest fabric by masons who were enthusiastic and hard-working,
he made immediate arrangements for its dedication. To this marriage of Christ and His church he invited King Edward himself of
holy memory, and his sister the queen, as well as leading men from
the whole of England: first Cynesige, archbishop of York, because
at that time the see of Canterbury was vacant;[4] then the other
bishops of both provinces whose names I have pleasure in listing at
this time as I have learned them from my predecessors, though I do
not remember their actual sees: they were Ælfwold, Hereman,
Leofric, William, Æthelmær, Leofwine, Wulfwig, Ælfwine,
Æthelric, Walter, and Giso, bishop of Cirencester.[5] There were

weight, twenty-six marks worth of the gold used, indicates that the embroidery was
lavish (Dodwell, *Anglo-Saxon Art*, p. 185).   [4] See above, p. xlii.
   [5] Giso was bishop of Wells, not Cirencester. For the other witnesses, see above,
p. xli.

subscribuntur, Eilnodus, Eilwinus, Wlfricus, Leuricus, Wlstanus,
fo. 93ʳ Etheluiz,ᵃ Ordricus, | Elsinus, Lefstanus, Edmundus et Sihtric.
Comites etᵇ regni primates, Elfgarus comes, Tostinus comes,
Lefwinus comes, Gierht comes,ᶜ Esegarus regie procurator aule,
qui et Anglice dictus stallere, id est regni uexillifer. Robertus
comes, domini regis cognatus, Radulfus regis aulicus, Bundinusᵈ
regis palatinus, Esebernus regis consanguineus, Rembaldus regis
cancellarius. Principes qui et barones[1] dicti sunt, Brichtricus,ᵉ
Elstanus, Elfgarus, et Brixi, Eilnothus, Esebernus, Edgip,ᶠ[2] Eadri-
cus, Ailmundus, Siwardus, Ethelwoldus, Alwinus,ᵍ Acurus
dapifer, et Ywingus dapifer regis, Godwinus regine dapifer, et
Doddo regis pre ceteris consanguinitate proximus,[3] Raulinus
cubiculariusʰ pre cunctis secretorum suorum in Domino Iesu
conscius.ⁱ Hos inuitatos et sagaci discretione conquisitos, quorum
fo. 93ᵛ quidam | oderant eum inuidia uel innata eis malitia quia non erat ei
similis in terra,[4] continuis octo diebus secum tenuit, cum omni
gloria et omnium donorum, ciborum,ʲ et potuum exquisitorum
opulentia, ita ut pro certo audierim ego a quibusdam qui hoc
acceperunt a patribus suis qui affuerunt, uasa magna, in conpitis
uiarum exposita discurrentibus, uino et medone plena ut haurirent
de pleno quicumque uellent.ᵏ

xvii. *De reliquiis quas dedit et abscondit Haroldus.*

Consummatis prima die dedicationi necessariis, antequam pran-
derent, in presentia domini regis et archiepiscopi Ginsi et epis-
corum, abbatum, comitum, et baronum prenominatorum, uocatisˡ
ad se Wlwino preposito et ecclesie canonicis, comes Haroldus
reliquiarum copiam fecit apponi, quas ipse multo labore inestima-
fo. 94ʳ bilique diligentia conquisierat;[5] sicut erat reuerende | faciei homo
et prestabilis eloquentie, coram positis fratribus ecclesie dixit:
'Quoniam a primeue natiuitatis obcecatione "auri sacra fames"[6]

ᵃ Ethelnix *H*   ᵇ etiam *C*   ᶜ Gierht comes *om. H*   ᵈ Dundinus *H*
ᵉ Brichtricus *H*; Brithricus *C*   ᶠ Edgyp *H*   ᵍ Ailwinus *H*   ʰ concu-
bicularius *H*   ⁱ contius *C*   ʲ cultorum *H*   ᵏ uellet *H*   ˡ uoca-
tis *om. C*

---

[1] The term *barones* is used anachronistically for the Old English thegns. The term
used in the charter is *principes*.
[2] *Edgip* appears to be a misreading of *Eadwig* in the charter.
[3] See above, p. xliii.
[4] An oblique reference to internecine quarrels among the English magnates in the

also the abbots whose names are here listed: Æthelnoth, Ælfwine, Wulfric, Leofric, Wulfstan, Æthelwig, Ordric, Æthelsige, Leofstan, Edmund, and Sihtric. Earls and magnates in the realm were: the earls Ælfgar, Tostig, Leofwine, and Gyrth; the magnates were Asgar, steward of the palace, called 'staller' in English (that is, the standard-bearer of the realm), Earl Robert, kinsman of the king, Raulf, king's chamberlain, Bondig, a thegn, Esbern, kinsman of the king, Regenbald, king's chancellor. The leading men, who were also called barons,[1] were Brihtric, Ælfstan, Ælfgar, Brixi, Æthelnoth, Esbern, Eadwig,[2] Eadric, Æthelmund, Siward, Æthelwold, Ælfwine, Adzur the steward, Yfing the king's steward, Godwine the queen's steward, Doddo, the closest kinsman of the king,[3] Raulin, head chamberlain who knew better than all others the secrets of the king in the Lord Jesus. These men, who had been selected and invited with careful discretion, he kept with him for eight days in all, though some of them disliked him out of envy or from personal malice because he had no equal in the land.[4] But they enjoyed all the glory and the abundance of all the gifts, and the choicest food and drink: indeed, I have certainly heard it from some who themselves learned it from their fathers who were present, that great bowls full of wine and mead were placed at crossroads so that any travellers who wished could take their fill.

17. *The relics which Harold gave and buried.*

When the essential arrangements for the dedication on that first day had been carried out, and before they had dined, Earl Harold had a large number of holy relics, which he had acquired himself through considerable labour and immense diligence,[5] set before them in the presence of his lord the king, Archbishop Cynesige, the bishops, abbots, earls, and barons previously mentioned, and the canons of the church and Wulwin the dean, who had been summoned before him. Harold, being a man of commanding appearance and surpassing eloquence, spoke as follows in the presence of the appointed brethren of the church: 'Since from the time of man's original blindness "a sacred hunger for gold"[6] has

---

last days of King Edward. Ælfgar was made earl of East Anglia in 1053 and translated to his father Leofric's earldom of Mercia in 1057; he was involved in two rebellions (*ASC* 1055, 1058 (C, D, E); see Fleming, *Kings and Lords*, pp. 52, 56).
[5] Rogers, 'Waltham relic-list'.   [6] Vergil, *Aeneid*, iii. 57.

usque hodie successiue descendit in filios diffidentie,[1] timeo si capsis istis aureis et argenteis commendentur iste sanctorum reliquie
preciose, quid[a] est "super aurum et lapidem preciosum multum et
dulciora super mel et fauum"[2] tollantur[b] ab ecclesia, superueniente
perfidorum uesania, et cum ipsis uasis fictilibus sacrosancta hec
alienantur auaritie estibus a malis successoribus, et cedant in usus
peccatorum, que multo labore et exercitio meo adquisita, Domino
dicari constituimus. Vnde si bene placitum est in oculis tuis, domine
mi rex, et principum tuorum, humi recordantur, signata luto et
latere in loco secreto omni homini occulto, nisi tantum uni fides cui
fo. 94ᵛ habeatur|tantum thesaurum occultandi; securius est enim fictilibus
carere quam tam sacre rei presidiis priuari.'

Placuit hoc regi consilium laudanti et omnibus qui aderant, et
assumpto ligno salutifere crucis[3] et per medium secto, partem
unam cum reliquis sanctorum presidiis mandant sarcofago, super-
edificantes struem lapidum, immanem maceriem, scilicet satis
humilem nullam prestare ualentem oculis intuentium tantorum
sacramentorum notitiam. Hiis autem sacris reliquiis scripto unius-
cuiusque presignato propria manu, dignum duxit magister Adelar-
dus, scribendo in libro capitulari, memoriale posteris tradere,[c]
quibus non datur libere accessus secretiora loci illius penetrare.[4]

xviii. *Qualiter rex Edwardus confirmauit dona comitis Haroldi.*[d]

Tanti igitur boni expertem nolens se beatus ille rex Edwardus,
fo. 95ʳ post assig|nata comitis Haroldi donaria, cum ea, ore proprio,
cunctis audientibus, et carta sua[5] litteris aureis scripta confirmas-
set, et propria crucem auream manu in eadem exarasset, de suo
contulit ecclesie in dotem Hicche, cum omnibus sibi pertinentibus
in terris, pratis, pascuis, et aquis,[6] et Lamhedere, sicut cautum

---

[a] et quid *H* [b] et tollantur *H* [c] cradere *c* [d] De excommunica-
tione Sancti Edwardi et omnium episcoporum Anglie *rubric in H*

---

[1] Cf. Eph. 2: 2. [2] Ps. 18: 11 (19: 10).
[3] The meaning is not clear, but most probably Harold had acquired among his relics
a supposed fragment of the True Cross. It cannot apply to the great cross on which the
imago Christi was fixed, which was in its place in the church on the eve of the battle of
Hastings, and which is never confused with the True Cross by the author. Cf. *De domino
ligno* in the relic list (Rogers, 'Waltham relic-list', p. 170).
[4] Miscellaneous records relating to the church treasures and ritual were copied into
monastic 'chapter books'; cf. the chapter book of Saint-Evroult (Paris, Bibliothèque
nationale, MS lat. 10062).

descended upon the sons of disobedience[1] from generation to generation up to this present time, I fear that, if these precious relics of the saints are entrusted to these reliquaries of gold and silver, something "far more valuable than gold or precious stones and sweeter than honey and the honeycomb"[2] may, through the prevailing madness of wicked men, be stolen from the church, and in these man-made vessels these holy things may be alienated through the greed of evil men in later generations, and put to the use of sinners. Yet these are things acquired by my own considerable toil and effort which I have decided to dedicate to the Lord. Therefore, if it meets with your approval, my lord king, and that of your chief men, let them be buried in the ground, sealed with clay, to lie hidden in a secret place concealed from all mankind except for the one man alone who is to be entrusted with the task of hiding this great treasure, for it is safer to be deprived of man-made vessels than to lose the protection of so sacred a thing.'

The king and all who were present approved and applauded this plan, and the wood of the Cross[3] which brings salvation was taken and cut down the middle: they committed one section, with the other protecting relics of the saints, to a tomb, building over it a heap of stones and around it a huge wall, though a quite plain one, which could prevent the eyes of onlookers from gaining knowledge of such holy things. Master Adelard, after writing down in his own hand a record of each one of these sacred relics, thought it right to pass on an account of this by writing it in a chapter book for their descendants who would not freely have access to penetrate the deeper secrets of that place.[4]

18. *King Edward confirmed Earl Harold's gifts.*

The blessed King Edward, not wishing to be excluded from this generous act, later confirmed in his own words in the hearing of everybody and by his own charter[5] written in letters of gold, the gifts which Earl Harold had assigned, and having drawn a gold cross on the charter with his own hand, then granted to the church as a gift from his own lands Hitchin with all its appurtenances in lands, meadows, pastures, and waters,[6] and in addition, Lambeth.

[5] See above, p. xxxviii.
[6] The chronicler slightly adapts the clause in the charter, which runs 'Hycche cum omnibus ad se pertinentibus campis. pascuis. pratis. siluis. et aquis.'

uideri potest in carta ipsius, ratum et inuiolabile uolens Deo permanere, ita dicens: 'Si uero aliquis successorum meorum, quod absit, de terris istis quicquam subtraxerit, uel subtrahi permiserit, et inde requisitus emendare noluerit, ei Deus iustus iudex regnum pariter auferat et coronam.'[1]

Archiepiscopus etiam et episcopi predicti, necnon et abbates, unanimiter sententiam domini regis confirmauerunt in hiis uerbis: 'Ego Ginsi Eboracensis archiepiscopus, una cum fratribus con-

fo. 95ᵛ secrationi ecclesie assistentibus | excommunicamus, et a liminibus sancte ecclesie matris sequestramus, et maledictione perpetua condempnamus omnes transgressores huius regie et consularis donationis et eorum et nostre confirmationis. Amen, in perpetuum fiat, fiat.'[2] Hiis ita expletis, post octauum diem unusquisque remeauit ad propria. Rex uero Edwardus Wintoniam iter flexit, celebraturus ibidem in proximo solempnitatem sancti spiritus die Pentecostes, ubi contigisse quiddam mirabile dictu scriptum uidimus, et auctenticorum[a] relatione didicimus.

xix. *De anulo*[3] *quem sanctus Iohannes remisit sancto Edwardo et obitu eius.*

Sedente eo pro tribunali die festo in aula regia, et prestolante processionem et episcoporum presentiam qui diadema regni applicarent regio capiti,[4] ex inprouiso contigit ciues .xii. quatuor ciuitatum Anglie quas precipuas | dicimus, Londin', Eborac',

fo. 96ʳ Wintoni', et Lincoln', regiam aulam intrare, comis et barbis more peregrinorum dependentibus,[5] habitu honesto et incessu graui, facie serena, uerecunda[b] tamen, qui procedentes usque ad gradum ante sedem regiam, flexo genu adorauerunt. Quorum unus sic ait:

ᵃ attenticorum *C*   ᵇ uerecundia *H*

---

[1] Cynesige's anathema must have been copied by the author from a draft of the charter made shortly after the ceremony of consecration; the royal anathema corresponds almost word for word with that in the royal charter, and may have been copied from either document. See above, pp. xxxvii–xliii.

[2] See above, p. xlii.

[3] A different version of the legend of the ring is found in an addition by Ailred of Rievaulx to Osbert of Clare's *Vita Edwardi* written about 1138 (Barlow, *VER*, p. xxxviii n. 107). This slightly different version may have been a legend circulating in the 12th cent.; there is no record of its existence before the development of the cult of King Edward at that time.

[4] Opinions have differed on whether the seasonal crown-wearings of the Norman

Desiring, as can be seen in the provisions of his charter, that it should be ratified and remain inviolable before God, he spoke these words: 'If any of my successors, God forbid, take anything from these lands or allow it to be taken, and then be unwilling to restore when requested to do so, may the just God, being his judge, likewise take away his kingdom and crown.'[1]

The archbishop and the aforementioned bishops, as well as the abbots, unanimously confirmed the condemnation proclaimed by their lord the King in the following words: 'I, Cynesige, archbishop of York, together with my brethren present at the consecration of the church, do excommunicate and banish from the threshold of holy Mother Church, and condemn with an everlasting curse, all who offend against this gift of the king and earl, and the confirmation made by them and us, and so be it, so be it for ever and ever, Amen.'[2] Eight days after these events were over, each one of them returned to his own home. King Edward journeyed to Winchester to celebrate there, in due course, the solemn feast of the Holy Spirit on the day of Pentecost. It was on this day that an event marvellous to relate took place; we have seen it written down and have learned about it from the report of trustworthy men.

19. *The ring[3] which St John sent to St Edward, and his death.*

On the feast day the king was sitting officially in the royal court awaiting the procession and the appearance of the bishops who were to place the royal crown upon the king's head.[4] Suddenly twelve citizens from the four leading cities of London, York, Winchester, and Lincoln entered the royal court; their hair and beards were long like those of pilgrims,[5] their clothing was sober and their gait dignified, and their countenances were serene, yet humble. They processed up the steps before the royal throne, knelt, and prostrated themselves before him. One of them spoke as follows:

kings were the continuation of a pre-Conquest custom or a Norman innovation. Martin Biddle, in a recent discussion of the subject ('Seasonal festivals and residence, Winchester, Westminster and Gloucester in the tenth to twelfth centuries', *ANS* viii (1986), 51–72), suggests (p. 58) that Edward the Confessor 'may on occasion have anticipated the practice of crown-wearing at great feasts'. Since this legend may not have been circulated until some time after the Conquest it does not provide evidence either way.

[5] It was customary for pilgrims, penitents, and prisoners to allow their hair to grow long.

'Domine rex, in cuius ditione presentis status regni et principum
eius firmitas solida manet et inuiolabilis uirtus, nos serui tui sancta
inuisere loca cupientes, et ob remedium animarum nostrarum
sanctorum suffragia inplorantes, ad uocem prophete dicentis, "in
diebus sanctorum affligetis animas uestras[1] quia ieiunia et uigilie
et sancte afflictiones humiliata corpora macerant, et maculata
corda purificant", eligimus miseratione diuina Ierosolimam per-
gere, sancte natiuitatis, passionis, resurrectionis, ascensionis, et |
fo. 96ᵛ sancti spiritus in apostolos missionis uestigia, corde et sincera
deuotione quoad potuimus adorare, incolumitatis tue firmitatem,
uite diuturnitatem, et regni prosperitatem, et animarum nostra-
rumᵃ salutem implorare.

'Vbi cum die quadam, uisitatis sacris in ciuitate locis, ascendere
uolentes Montem Oliuarum, ubi ab humilitate nostra ad summa
celorum fastigia ascendit Dominus, in decliuo montis obuiam
habuimus processionem, sicut in diebus solempnibus, ordinate
incedentem cruce, turribulo, ceroferariis, subdiacono et diacono
precedentibus, subsequente conuentu honestissimo, sacerdote
postremo, quos cum intuiti essemus clara luce circa tertiam diei
horam non sine admiratione sic incedere, dixit nobis ille ultimus,
sacerdotalibus pre ceteris indutus: "Vnde estis, ad quid uenistis,
fo. 97ʳ quorsum tenditis, | que uos genuit terra, et quid animi uobis est in
scopuloso hoc regno multa asperitate discreto?"[2] Ad quem ego,
licet sodalium non preminentior, respondi: "Angli quidem sumus
uestre sanctitatis serui, sacra inuisere loca cupientes; hinc ultra
procedere non disponimus; repedare illuc unde uenimus, Dei
nutu, desideramus; uestrarum orationum benefitiis attolli suppli-
citer postulamus." Respondens autem uir sanctus: "Vere quidem
Angli," subintulit, "nitentes ut angeli;[3] benedicat uos Deus et
gratie sue in uobis dona multiplicet. Numquid regem habetis aut
quo nomine censetur?" Cui respondimus: "Regem habemus,
Edwardum nomine, uirum probate uite et sanctitatis immense, in
terre sue strenuum regimine,ᵇ uirum iustum et prudentem, et ad
fo. 97ᵛ omnimoda regni moderamina regibus | aliis preminentem."

'Audito quidem nomine uestro uir sanctus ille subintulit:

ᵃ nostrarum *om.* H   ᵇ in regimine H

---

[1] Actually the Pentateuch (cf. Lev. 16: 29, 23: 27).
[2] The consecutive questions asked by a host to a guest are a rhetorical device of classical epic; cf. Vergil, *Aeneid*, viii. 112–14.
[3] Cf. Bede, *HE* ii, 1, pp. 134, 135.

'Lord king, under whose sway the state of the present realm and the strength of its leading men remain secure, and its virtue inviolable, we your servants, desiring to visit the holy places, and pleading for the intercession of the saints for the salvation of our souls, chose by divine mercy to travel to Jerusalem in response to the words of a prophet saying "On saints days you shall afflict your souls[1] with fasting, vigils, and holy chastisement, for these humble and mortify the flesh, and purify the sin-stained soul." Jerusalem is the place of the Holy Birth, the Passion, the Resurrection, and the Ascension, and where the Holy Spirit was sent to the apostles. We went to worship with all our hearts and with pure devotion, and to pray for your continued safety and length of life, for the prosperity of your realm and the salvation of our souls.

'Here, one day after we had visited holy places in the city, we wished to climb the Mount of Olives where the Lord ascended from the humility of our human condition to the highest vaults of Heaven. On the slopes of the Mount we met a procession which, as was usual on feast days, was making its way in ordered fashion, with a cross, a thurible, acolytes, a sub-deacon and deacon at the head, and a most reverend company behind it with the priest at the end. When we had watched them with a great sense of wonder thus processing in the bright sunshine—it was about nine o'clock in the morning—the man at the end of the procession, dressed in priestly robes finer than those of the others, spoke to us in these words: "Where are you from? Why have you come here? Where are you making for? What is your native land, and what do you intend to do in this rocky kingdom noted for its ruggedness?"[2] It was I who replied to him, though I held no position of pre-eminence over my companions: "We are indeed English, servants of your Holiness, who wish to visit the holy places; we do not intend to go any further, but desire, God willing, to go back whence we came, and we humbly pray that we may be sustained by the support of your prayers." In reply, the holy man added: "Truly, you Angles shine like angels;[3] may God bless you and shower upon you the gifts of his grace. Do you not have a king? If so, what is his name?" Our reply to him was this: "We have a king named Edward, a man of integrity and of extraordinary holiness, vigorous in his rule over his land, a just and learned man who excels other kings in every aspect of governance of the realm."

'On hearing your name mentioned, that holy man continued:

"Qualem uos dicitis, talem probat eum Deus, quia Domino con-
placuit in eo, quod nouiter probabit experimento. Obtestor uos
per misericordiam Dei, propter quam adipiscendam multo labore
et sudore hucusque uenistis, quod sugeratis ei, ex parte dilecti sui
Iohannis ewangeliste, quod preparet se huic collegio interesse,
quod sic futurum infra presentem annum preparauit Deus diligenti[a] se. Nos enim diurno et nocturno beate uirginis obsequio
ministrare constituti sumus, a Domino et ipsius sepulcro in
Iosaphat[1] serui addicti [b]cum eiusdem uirginis immaculato filio
Domino nostro Iesu Christo in regno celesti manemus[b] in perpetuum ubi gaudium inestimabile, pax et delectatio inenarrabilis,
interna refectio et[c] leticia est[d] sine fine mansura. Huius amenitatis
socius euocatur[e] Edwardus a Christo salutari suo, quia uirgo
fo. 98[r] electus | a Domino uirgo in euum permanebit huic, collocandus
consortio. Si uero uestris fidem non habuerit, hiis saltem credat
intersignis, quod in dedicatione ecclesie de Claueringes[2] ob
honorem mei, dum proteruus[f] assisteret ei exactor elemosine, nec
haberet quod daret illi, et ille indesinenter instaret ut benefaceret
ei causa Dei et sancti Iohannis ewangeliste, cum non haberet ad
presens quid tribueret, audito nomine Iohannis, anulum quem
habebat insignem supra modum instanti tribuit michi, et sic ab
oculis eius et omnium hominum usque hodie euanui. Hunc autem
anulum fidei nostre signaculum perferetis ad eum, et si non
simplicibus uerbis, hiis autem credat inditiis." Hec mandata
perferenda ad uos, domine mi rex, ab ore Iohannis ewangeliste
accepimus; hec comonitoria ab ipso audiuimus, et anulum inter
fo. 98[v] uos | fidei signaculum deferimus.'

Quem cum respexisset in manu deferentis et ueris inditiis sic
esse cognouisset, humi prostratus gratias egit Deo et seruo suo
Iohanni, quibus et ipse militauit tribus mensibus; postea in
senectute bona, appositus ad patres suos, obdormiuit in Domino.[3]
Dissoluta igitur huius habitationis domo, domum non manu-
factam accepit rex iste gloriosus in celis, quam sibi cooperante Dei

---

[a] diligentibus *H*   [b-b] *C H692 (from marginal gloss)*; om. *H*   [c] est *H*
[d] est *later insertion in C*   [e] euocatus *H*   [f] *marginal gloss* importunus *C*

---

[1] Another form of 'Jehosaphat', a valley identified with the valley of the Kidron: a
monastic foundation was associated with it as early as the 6th cent. and a late 12th-cent.
monastery bore the name of St Mary of Josaphat; *IBC* ii. 816.
[2] The church of Clavering (Essex) is dedicated to St Clement. The author may be
thinking of the church of St John the Evangelist at Havering, which was a royal manor.

"God is proving this man to be such as you say, and so the Lord has decided to test him in a new way. I beg you by the mercy of God (to obtain which you have come all this way with much sweat and labour), to urge him, out of love for his beloved Evangelist John, to prepare himself to join this company, for this is what God has prepared during the present year for the one who loves him. We have been appointed by the Lord to conduct divine service for the Blessed Virgin day and night, and, dedicated as servants to her sepulchre in Josaphat[1] for ever, we dwell with the spotless Son of the same Virgin, our Lord Jesus Christ, in the kingdom of Heaven where boundless joy and unspeakable peace and delight, inner refreshment and happiness will last for ever. Edward is called by Christ his Saviour to share in His blessedness for, chosen by the Lord to be celibate, he will remain celibate for ever to dwell amongst this company. If he does not trust your words, then let him at least believe the following sign as evidence of truth. When he was dedicating the church of Clavering[2] in my honour, an importunate beggar was standing near him asking for alms, but he had nothing to give him. However, he was pressed insistently by the beggar to give him something for the sake of God and St John the Evangelist, but although he had no alms at hand to give him, when he heard the name of John, he bestowed on me—for it was I who was pressing him so hard—a valuable ring, which he had, and then I vanished from his and everyone else's sight until today. You are to take this ring to him as a sign of our trustworthiness, and if he cannot believe our simple words let him trust this evidence." These were the commands, my lord King, which we received from the lips of John the Evangelist that we had to bring to you. We heard these words of exhortation from John himself, and we set the ring before you as evidence of the truth.'

When the king looked at the ring in the hand of the man who had brought it, and recognized it as true evidence, he bowed himself to the ground and gave thanks to God and his servant John, and he served them as their knight for three months. After that, being of a ripe old age, he fell asleep in the Lord and was gathered unto his fathers.[3] So it was that the king, freed from his bodily habitation and glorious in the heavens, entered into that house not made with

[3] The author's chronology is telescoped at this point; not only does he place this episode very shortly after King Edward granted the Waltham charter (1062), but he states that his death occurred only three months after the restoration of the ring (Ailred of Rievaulx said six months).

gratia, manu, lingua fabrefecit in terris, ubi quod iam sitiuit inter-
num, gustat eternum, decoratus una stola securusque de reliqua.

xx. *De electione et coronatione. Et de inclinatione capitis sancte crucis, et de*
prostratione regis Haroldi in bello.

Post obitum itaque sanctissimi regis, comes Haroldus unanimi
omnium consensu in regem eligitur, quia non erat eo prudentior in
terra, armis strenuus magis, legum terre sagatior, in omni genere
fo. 99ʳ probita|tis cultior, ita ut huic electioni non possent contradicere
qui eum summo odio persecuti fuissent usque ad tempora illa,
quoniam tanto operi adeo insignem in omnibus non genuerit
Anglia. Rex igitur consecratus a Stigando, Dorobernensi archipre-
sule,[1] quod prius dilexerat non potuit odisse.

Veruntamen ecclesiam Walthamensem ampliori quam prius
amplexatus dilectione, multa donariorum uenustate cepit eam
ampliare, ita ut postea nullatenus sine multorum munerum
oblatione uellet etiam illam sedemᵃ uisitare. Quod et accepi ab ore
senioris sacriste Turkilli quem et uidere duobus annis antequam
moreretur merui,[2] et postea interesse cum ceteris fratribus eius
humationi. Breui tempore rex factus prefuit ecclesie nostre, nam
fo. 99ᵛ insidiantibus ei perfidis Nor|mannorum uersutiis quia filiam
Willelmi ducis Normannorum nuptui traditam ducere contemp-
sit;[3] rediens a Ponte Belli quod a bello cognomen accepit,[4] ibi cum
Tostino fratre suo multam stragem inimicorum faciens,[5] de
hostium multitudine nobiliter triumphauit. Inde paucis sibi
adiunctis, nam omnes fere in diuersas partes secesserant, Waltham
rediit ubi de applicatione Normannorum, nimis ueridica nar-
ratione, nuntium suscepit,[6] et eis obuiam ire subito disponit
nullius admissa prepeditione; nam ab omnibus consultum est ei

ᵃ sedem illam *H*

---

[1] This is in accordance with the Norman view that Harold was crowned by the
excommunicate archbishop Stigand; it represents a hardening of the tradition hostile to
Harold. For different versions see Orderic, ii. 138 n. 1.
[2] Since the author entered the college *c.* 1124, Turkill must have died *c.* 1126, sixty
years after Harold's death.
[3] There are different versions of Harold's alleged betrothal to a daughter of William
the Conqueror; see William of Poitiers, *Gesta Guillelmi*, p. 230; Eadmer, *Hist. Nov.*, p. 7;
Orderic, ii. 136; Malmesbury, *Gesta Regum*, ii. 333; and see D. C. Douglas, *William the
Conqueror* (London, 1964), App. C, pp. 393–5; Freeman, *Norman Conquest*, iv, Appendix,
Note O.

hands which, by the help of God's grace, he had fashioned on earth by his words and actions. The place for which he had already inwardly thirsted he tasted for evermore, adorned with one robe, for he needed no other.

20. *The election of a king and the coronation. The holy cross bows its head, and King Harold is vanquished in battle.*

After the death of this most saintly king, therefore, Earl Harold was elected king by unanimous consent, for there was no one in the land more knowledgeable, more vigorous in arms, wiser in the laws of the land or more highly regarded for his prowess of every kind. So those who had been his chief enemies up to this time could not oppose this election, for England had not given birth to a man as distinguished as he in all respects to undertake such a task. So after being crowned king by Stigand, archbishop of Canterbury,[1] he could not have hated what he previously favoured.

And, indeed, he now showed a greater affection for the church at Waltham than before, and began to adorn it further with many fine gifts; indeed, he never thereafter visited that place without wanting to bestow many gifts upon it. I heard this from the lips of the old sacristan Turkill whom I was privileged to see two years before he died[2] and later to be present with the brethren at his burial. But it was only for a short time after he became king that he was patron of our church, for he was cunningly tricked by the perfidious Normans because he had refused to marry the daughter of William of Normandy.[3] Returning from Battlebridge, a name the place received from the battle itself,[4] where with his brother Tostig he had slaughtered a large number of his enemies,[5] he nobly triumphed over the forces of the enemy. Then with a few companions—for almost all his men had departed to different regions—he returned to Waltham. There he received a message about the landing of the Normans,[6] news that was only too true, and straightway he decided to go and meet them, allowing nobody to stop him. In fact,

[4] Gaimar (v. 5227) refers to Stamford Bridge as 'punt de la bataille'. See also *Orbis Latinus*, iii. 180–1.

[5] The author here represents Tostig as fighting on the same side as Harold, possibly through a pious wish to avoid impugning the founder of Waltham as a fratricide.

[6] Florence of Worcester (i. 227) says that Harold heard the news of the Norman invasion at Stamford Bridge and then hurried south; this is far more likely to be true than Orderic's statement (Orderic, ii. 171) that he heard it at London.

Tostinum, Gerth, et Bundinum,[1] et reliquos qui secesserant[2] expectare, set nimis preceps et de uirtute sua presumens, credebat se inualidos et inpremunitos Normannos expugnare antequam a Normannia gens subsecutiua in presidium eorum | succresceret; set hiis auspitiis defuit uirtus omnipotentis.

fo. 100[r]

Nam mane facto ecclesiam sancte crucis ingrediens et reliquas quas apud se habebat in capella sua repositas altari superponens, uotum uouit quod si successus prosperos sub euentu belli prestaret ei Dominus, copiam prediorum et multitudinem clericorum Deo ibidem seruiturorum, ecclesie conferret, et se Deo seruiturum[a] amodo quasi seruum empticium sponderet. Clero igitur eum comitante et processione precedente, ueniunt ad ualuas templi ubi conuersus ad crucifixum, rex ille sancte cruci[b] deuotus, ad terram in modum crucis prosternens se, pronus orauit. Contigit autem interea miserabile dictu et a seculis incredibile. Nam imago crucifixi, que prius erecta ad superiora respiciebat, cum se rex humiliaret in terram, | demisit uultum, quasi tristis; signum quidem prescium futurorum! Hoc se uidisse contestatus est Turkillus sacrista et multis intimasse, dum et ipse colligeret et reconderet que[3] altari superposuit rex benefitia. Ab eius ore ego hoc suscepi, et multorum assertione prestantium uirorum qui oculis suis caput imaginis erectum uiderunt, set nulli preter Turkillum demissionis horam nouerunt.[4]

fo. 100[v]

Viso autem hoc infausto auspicio, multo dolore correpti, duos fratres de ecclesia precipuos et maiores natu, Osegodum Cnoppe et Ailricum Childemaister, in comitatu regis miserunt ad prelium ut cognitis rei euentibus, de corpore regis et suorum ecclesie deuotorum curam agerent et, si fortuna sic daret, cadauera reportarent.

Modico stipatus agmine[5] rex properat ad expugnandas gentes |

---

[a] seruiturorum C (*later hand in marg.*); seruiencium H   [b] crucis H

[1] Bondig was one of King Edward's stallers; after the Conquest he attested a charter of King William and was the recipient of one of his writs (*Regesta*, i, nos. 18, 23).

[2] Cf. Malmesbury, *Gesta Regum*, i. 281–2.

[3] Turkill collected together the precious relics presumably to prevent their being confiscated by the Normans.

[4] For the story of Harold's visit to Waltham before the battle of Hastings, see above, pp. xliii, xlvii. Rogers, 'Waltham relic-list', pp. 159–60, suggests that this 'could be rationalized as a reference to a mid-eleventh-century refashioning of the *crucifixus* to make it accord more with the naturalism of contemporary Ottonian and Anglo-Saxon images'. For other examples of crucifixes that behaved as though they were alive, see Raw, *AS Iconography*, p. 18.

everyone advised him to wait for Tostig, Gyrth, and Bondig,[1] and the rest who had gone back home,[2] but he was headstrong and trusted too much in his own courage; he believed he would be attacking a weak and unprepared force of Normans before reinforcements from Normandy could increase their strength; but the power of the Almighty was not with him, as the following omens show.

He had entered the church of the Holy Cross in the early morning, and placing upon the altar relics which he had with him in his chapel, he made a vow that if the Lord granted him success in the outcome of the war he would endow the church with a large number of estates as well as many clerks to serve God in that place, and he promised to serve God in the future like a purchased slave. Accompanied by the clergy, and with a procession leading the way, he came to the doors of the church where, turning towards the crucifix, the king in devotion to the holy cross stretched himself out on the ground in the form of a cross and prayed. Then occurred an event pitiable to relate and incredible from an earthly point of view. When the king bowed low to the ground the image of the crucified one, which had previously been looking directly ahead above him, now bowed its head as if in sorrow, a sign portending what was to happen! Turkill, the sacristan, testified that he had seen this while he was himself collecting together[3] and putting away the gifts which the king had placed on the altar, and that he told many people about it. I heard this from his very lips, and it was confirmed by many bystanders who with their own eyes saw the head of the figure upright, though none of them except Turkill knew the moment it had bowed.[4]

When they saw this ill-omen, grief-stricken they sent to the battle two of the elder brethren from the church, Osgod Cnoppe and Æthelric Childemaister, to join the king's retinue and ascertain the outcome of the conflict. They were to have responsibility for the king's body and those of his men devoted to the church; if things turned out badly they were to bring back their corpses.

Thronged by a small band of men,[5] the king hastened to drive

---

[5] This seems to reinforce the previous statement that Harold refused to wait for much of his army. Reports were probably confusing; *ASC* (1066 D) said that Harold assembled a large army, while Florence of Worcester (i. 227) claimed that he engaged the enemy before a third of his army was in battle order. For a recent assessment of the battle, see R. Allen Brown, 'The Battle of Hastings', *ANS* iii (1981), 1–21.

fo. 101ʳ exteras, heu nimis animosus, minus quidem quam expediret circumspectus, propriis quidem magis quam suorum confidens uiribus. Set 'frangit Deus omne superbum',[1] nec diuturnum extat[a] hominis edifitium, cui non est ipse Deus fundamentum. Fit congressus belli; cadunt hinc inde milites proceri; gens effera Normannorum, peruicatie non ignara, huiusmodi calamitatibus magis assueta quam gens nostra, penetrant cuneos nichil preter sanguinem regis sitientes.[2]

Quid multis moror? Indultus est effere genti de hoste triumphus. Cadit rex ab hoste fero, gloria regni, decus cleri, fortitudo militie, inermium clipeus, certantium firmitas, tutamen debilium, consolatio desolatorum, indigentium reparator, procerum gemma.

fo. 101ᵛ Non potuit de pari contendere, qui | modico stipatus agmine quadruplo congressus exercitui, sorti se dedit ancipiti.

'Vt quid, Deus, reppulisti in finem, iratus est furor tuus super oues pascue tue? Memor esto congregationis tue'[3] quam in honorem[b] passionis tue tibi dicauit rex ille nobilis in Waltham, seruus tibi factus humilis, non sua tantum largiens, set et se ipsum exinaniens[c] ut seruum tibi se constitueret, et sancte passionis tue preconem et exactissimum ministrum exhiberet. Numquid obliuio cadit[d] in Deum? Numquid obliuioni, tanquam mortuus, datus est ille a corde tuo, bone Iesu, cui non fuit satis sua tibi et suorum exquisitissime benefitia conferre munificentiarum, set de remotis mundi partibus querere; amator ille decoris domus tue, quo ipsam

fo. 102ʳ redimire posset et multiphariis be|nefitiorum bonis attollere. Set quid restat, plange, Waltham, et luge, et exue te uestibus iocunditatis; induere cinere et cilitio, quia priuauit te Dominus sponso iocunditatis tue. 'Deducant oculi lacrimas per diem et noctem',[4] et 'non taceat pupilla oculi tui',[5] quoniam instat tibi tempus uiduitatis, tempus desolationis quale non fuit tibi ab initio.

Rex gloriose, cedat ad commodum anime tue quod tanto affectu,

---

[a] prestat C (*later hand in marg.*) H   [b] honore H   [c] *lacuna before* exinaniens H   [d] cadet H

---

[1] Cf. Prudentius, *Psychomachia*, 285: 'Desine grande loqui; frangit Deus omne superbum.'

[2] The *Carmen* also asserts (p. 34) the determination of the Normans to kill the king, and though the scene purporting to describe the slaying of Harold has justly been called 'the most improbable scene in the whole poem' (R. H. C. Davis, 'The *Carmen de Hastingae Proelio*', *EHR* xciii (1978), 241–61), there must have been a hope that he would fall in battle. Most sources are more reticent; but William must have been aware that a captive Harold would be a lasting danger.

out these foreigners but, alas, too boldly and too rashly to advance his cause, and trusting more in his own personal strength than that of his men. But 'God breaks all who are proud',[1] and a man's bodily habitation does not last long if God is not its foundation. The battle commenced; the leading men fell this side and that, and the fierce race of Normans, no strangers to stubborn resistance and more accustomed than our race to onslaughts of this kind, penetrated our ranks, thirsting above all for the blood of the king.[2]

Why do I delay any longer telling the story? Victory over its enemy was granted to that savage race. The king who was the glory of the realm, the darling of the clergy, the strength of his soldiers, the shield of the defenceless, the support of the distressed, the protector of the weak, the consolation of the desolate, the restorer of the destitute, and the pearl of princes, was slain by his fierce foe. He could not fight an equal contest for, accompanied by only a small force, he faced an army four times as large as his; but he submitted to his fate, whatever it might be.

'Why, O God, have you turned your anger against the sheep of your pasture and cast them off for ever? Remember your flock'[3] which the noble king dedicated to you at Waltham in honour of your Passion. He became your humble servant, not only giving generously of his own possessions, but also emptying himself to devote his life to your service and to show himself to be a herald and devoted minister of your holy Passion. But surely God does not forget? And you, sweet Jesus, have not consigned him to oblivion separated from your love as though dead, for he did not stop at bestowing upon you his own possessions and the choicest of gifts from his own people, but sought them from the furthest regions of the world. Devoted to the beauty of your house, he did everything he could to surround it with beauty, and to honour it with the many and varied gifts he bestowed upon it. But hereafter, Waltham, grieve and mourn, shed your garments of joy and put on sackcloth and ashes, for the Lord has deprived you of your hope of joy. 'Let your eyes shed tears day and night',[4] and 'let them know no rest',[5] for your time of bereavement is at hand, a time of desolation such as you have not known from the beginning.

O glorious king, may it redound to the good of your soul that

³ Ps. 73 (74): 1.
⁴ Jer. 14: 17.
⁵ Lam. 2: 18.

tanta deuotione, tantaque cordis et spiritus contricione[a] exultauit anima tua in crucis sacre cumulandis honoribus; retribuat tibi omnium bonorum largitor pro bonis ecclesie collatis largam benedictionem; exaudiat te Dominus in die tribulationis, memor[b] omnis sacrificii tui, et holocausta tua igne spiritus sui plenius accendantur; tribuat tibi quod magis expediat anime tue, | et omne consilium salutis perpetue in te confirmet. Inpleat Dominus omnes petitiones et exaudiat quas pro te dirigunt ad ipsum filii Walthamensis cenobii. Quod quidem futurum non ambigo, si enim sileat lingua nostra, orant pro te benefitia tua, et eorum affectus quos ipsis benefitiis magis pensat Deus, et det tibi crucifixus ille dulcis Iesus quicquid optari queat felitius.

fo. 102ᵛ *(margin)*

> Heu cadis hoste fero rex a duce rege futuro,
> Par paris in gladio milite cum ualido.
> Firmini[1] iusti lux est tibi luce Calixti[2]
> Pronior, hinc superas, hinc superatus eras.
> Ergo tibi requiem deposcat uterque perhennem,
> Sicque precetur eum quod colit omne Deum.

xxi. *Qualiter canonici petunt a uictore corpus Haroldi; querunt, inueniunt, et sepeliunt.*

Post miserabiles belli euentus et infaustum omen certantium, quid animi, quid angoris, quidue | supremi doloris fuerit fratribus predictis Osegodo et Ailrico qui fatales[c] hos regis euentus secuti fuerant a longe ut uiderent finem, pensare poterit cuius animo hoc fixum sit, 'O uos qui transitis per uiam attendite et uidete si est dolor sicut dolor meus.'[d][3] Necessitate tamen urgente, etsi timore obstante, ducem adeunt pedibus humiliati; precibus lacrimas addunt dicentes: 'Dux generose, nos serui tui, omni solatio destituti (utinam sic et uita presenti!), exploraturi huc destinati sumus euentus belli a fratribus quos rex iste defunctus[e] in ecclesia Walthamensi constituerat, set successibus uestris prouidens

fo. 103ʳ *(margin)*

---

[a] contrione *C*   [b] memor sit *H*   [c] fatale *CH*   [d] noster *H*
[e] defuntus *C*

---

[1] St Firmin of Amiens' feast day was 25 September, the day the battle of Stamford Bridge was fought.
[2] St Calixtus' feast day was 14 October, the day the battle of Hastings was fought.
[3] Lam. 1: 12.

your spirit rejoiced in so great a love, so great a devotion, and so great a contrition of heart and spirit in heaping honours upon the holy cross; may the bestower of all good things repay you with his great blessing for the good things you have bestowed upon the church; may the Lord hear you in the day of tribulation, mindful of all your sacrifice, and may your burnt offering be kindled the more fully with the fires of his Spirit; may he grant you whatever is more expedient for your soul, and confirm in you all knowledge of eternal salvation. May the Lord fulfil all your petitions and hear those which the sons of the community at Waltham make to him on your behalf. I do not doubt what your lot will be, for even if our tongues were silent, your gifts would cry out on your behalf, as would the love of those whom God regards more highly than those very gifts; and may sweet Jesus, the crucified one, grant you fully all your heart's desires.

> Alas, O king, you fall to a fierce foe, a duke and future king,
> Equal to him in combat, each a valiant knight.
> Firmin the just's day[1] favoured you, for then you were the victor,
> Not so Calixtus' day,[2] for then you were the vanquished.
> So may both saints implore eternal rest for you,
> And all that worships God thus pray to Him.

21. *The canons ask the Conqueror for Harold's body. They seek, find, and bury it.*

After the unhappy outcome of the battle, with its bad omen for those who fought in it, the man who can recall the verse 'O you who pass by, look and see if there is any sorrow like my sorrow'[3] will be able to appreciate what feelings of anguish and sorrow the brethren Osgod and Æthelric had to endure, who had followed the king's doomed fortunes from afar that they might see his end. Compelled by necessity, however, though their fear made them hesitant, they approached the duke, humbling themselves before his feet. Tearfully they addressed and entreated him: 'Noble duke, we your servants, bereft of all solace (would that we were bereft now of our lives!) were sent here to observe the outcome of the war by our brethren whom the dead king had appointed to the church at Waltham, but our master who provided for us has, because of

Dominus sublatus est de medio qui consolabatur nos, cuius presidiis necnon et stipendiis Deo militabant[a] quos ipse in ecclesia instituit; rogamus, domine, et contestamur te per gratiam tibi

diuinitus collatam et pro remedio animarum | omnium eorum qui in presenti causa uestri expleuerunt dies suppremos, quod liceat nobis in beneplacito uestro corpora tollere et nobiscum libere deportare domini regis fundatoris et institutoris ecclesie nostre, necnon et eorum qui ob reuerentiam ipsius sepulture locum elegerunt aput nos ut ipsorum presidiis munita firmior maneat status ecclesie et perpetuitas illibata.'

Quorum precibus et irriguis fletibus egregius dux ille motus, 'Rex,' inquid, 'uester fidei sue religionis immemor, etsi dignas transgressionis ad presens exsoluerit penas,[1] non meruit sepulture benefitio priuari. Quoniam regimen tante sedis, quocumque modo adeptus, diem consummauit rex dictus, paratus sum ob illius reuerentiam et salutem defunctorum qui causa mei relictis uxoribus et hereditatibus huic conquistioni[b] coadiutores animas

exalauer|unt, ecclesiam et ordinem monasticum centum monacorum instituere qui perhenniter eorum saluti animarum inuigilent, et ipsum regem uestrum in ecclesia eadem debito cum honore pre ceteris sublimare et ob ipsius reuerentiam locum amplioribus benefitiis augere.'[2]

Ad quem fratres illi, multo talia promittentis solatio conS confortati, 'Non,' inquid, 'magne rex future, annue precibus supplicantium ut successibus suis gaudeat generosa sublimitas tua, et has .x. marcas auri ex benefitio defuncti in usus tuorum digneris suscipere, et corpus ad locum quem instituit ipse remittere ut benefitio corporis exhilarati, de morte ipsius plurimam nos gaudeamus suscepisse consolationem, et posteris nostris presens in ecclesia tumuli structura perpetuum sit monimentum.'[3]

Compatiens igitur dux ille gloriosus, ut erat miseri|cordis animi et pronioris ad exaudiendum propter successus, quia dederat ei Dominus de hoste triumphum, annuit uotis eorum, spernens et

---

[a] militabamus *H*   [b] conquisitione *C*

---

[1] The reference seems to be to the oath Harold was alleged to have sworn in 1064 to support William's claim to the English throne. There is general agreement in the sources that Harold took an oath of some kind, but authorities differ on its exact nature (Freeman, *Norman Conquest*, iii, Appendix, Note U).

[2] If this is intended as a reference to Battle Abbey, the Chronicle is the only source apart from the Battle Chronicle to suggest that William's decision to found an abbey

your victory, been taken from us. He used to console us, and it was under his protection, indeed, and through his endowments that those whom he established in the church served God. We ask you, master, indeed we urge you, through the grace bestowed upon you by the divine will, and for the salvation of the souls of all who have lost their lives in this present cause of yours, to allow us at your good pleasure to remove and take with us without let or hindrance the body of our lord the king, the founder and originator of our church, together with the bodies of the men who, out of reverence for the place itself, have chosen a place of burial amongst us. We ask this that the standing of the church might be established more firmly under their protection, and its continuance be assured.'

The noble duke was moved by their entreaties and by the tears they shed, and he replied, 'Your king neglected his good faith, yet, though he has now paid the due penalty of his sin,[1] he has not deserved to be deprived of the benefit of burial. Now that your king, who gained command over this great church by whatever means, has ended his days, I am prepared, out of respect for him and for the salvation of the dead who left wives and estates in my cause and died in my service in the course of this conquest, to establish a church and a monastic community of one hundred monks who will pray without ceasing for the salvation of those men's souls; and in that same church to exalt your king himself above all others with due honour and, out of respect for him, to enrich the place with large endowments.'[2]

The brethren, though greatly comforted and consoled by such promises, replied, 'No, great king to be, grant the prayers of suppliants that your noble highness may rejoice in his victory, and that you may deign to accept these ten marks of gold from the endowment of the dead king for the use of your men, and to return his body to the place which he himself founded so that we, happy in the gift of his body, may rejoice that we have received great consolation out of his death, and that the building of a tomb in the church in our own time may be a perpetual memorial for our descendants.'[3]

Accordingly that glorious duke showed them compassion characteristic of a mind that is merciful and more prone to listen because of victory, for the Lord had permitted him his triumph

was taken in 1066; see Eleanor Searle, *The Chronicle of Battle Abbey* (OMT, 1980), pp. 20–1.

[3] For the various versions of Harold's burial, see above, pp. xliv–xlv.

pro nichilo oblatum reputans aurum. 'Si quid autem,' inquit, 'uobis defuerit in expensis ad exhibenda funeralia offitia, uel itineri uestro quocumque modo necessaria, habundanter uobis exhiberi precipimus, pacem et omnimodam tranquillitatem a commilitionibus exercitus nostri uobis per omnia indulgemus.'

Gaudio igitur inestimabili fratres confortati, currunt ad cadauera, et uertentes ea huc et illuc, domini regis corpus agnoscere non ualentes, quia corpus hominis exangue[a] non consueuit mortuum formam prioris status frequenter exprimere; unicum placuit remedium, ipsum Osegodum domum redire et mulierem

fo. 105[r] quam ante sumptum regimen Anglorum dilexerat, | Editham cognomento Swanneshals, quod gallice sonat 'collum cigni', secum adducere que, domini regis quandoque cubicularia,[1] secretiora in eo signa nouerat ceteris amplius, ad ulteriora intima secretorum admissa, quatinus ipsius noticia certificarentur secretis inditiis qui exterioribus non poterant, quia statim letali uulnere confosso, quicquid in eo regalis erat insignii duci deportatum est, signum scilicet prostrationis regie, quoniam consuetudinis erat antique, et adhuc credimus moderne, in regum expugnatione uel castrorum captione magnis eos donari muneribus qui primi possent regis conum deicere et regi offerre, uel primus castro expugnato regis uexillum, precipue ipsius castri munitioni eminentis.

Quam cum adduxisset Osegodus et inter strages mortuorum

fo. 105[v] pluribus inditiis ipsa | corpus regis Haroldi designasset, aptatum feretro, multis heroum Normannie comitatus honorem corpori exibentibus usque ad Pontem Belli,[2] qui nunc dicitur, ab ipsis fratribus et multa superuenientium copiositate Anglorum qui audierant eorum imminens[b] excidium, quia nunquam fuit Anglis cognata Normannorum sotietas, cum magno honore corpus Waltham deductum sepelierunt, ubi usque hodie, quicquid

[a] exangues C   [b] eminens H

---

[1] Edith was Harold's handfast wife; for their children see *Handbook of British Chronology*, ed. E. B. Fryde *et al.* (Royal Historical Society, 3rd edn., 1986), p. 29; Emma Mason, *St Wulfstan of Worcester* (Oxford, 1990), pp. 220, 226. It is possible that she was the *quaedam concubina Heraldi* who held four houses in Canterbury (*DB* i. 2), or Edith *pulchra* who held land in Herts. and Cambs. (*DB* i. 134, 137, 190).

[2] The site of the battle had no widely-known name before the town of Battle grew up around the abbey. Orderic called it 'Senlac' (sandy lake), the name adopted by Freeman. *Pons belli* is the name the author had given for the battle of Stamford Bridge, and the repetition here may be simply an error.

over his enemy. He therefore granted them their requests, rejecting the gold offered to him, considering it of no consequence. He
continued, 'If you need anything towards the expenses for carrying
out the funeral ceremony, or have any needs at all for your journey,
we are giving orders for these to be fully satisfied. We grant you
peace and complete freedom from molestation by the knights of
our army in all you have to do.'

And so the brethren were strengthened by feelings of extraordinary joy. They hastened to the dead bodies and, though turning them over on this side and that, they were unable to recognize
the body of the king. This is because the body of a man when dead
and drained of blood does not usually have the same appearance as
when alive. They decided that there was only one solution, for
Osgod himself to return home and to bring back with him the
woman whom the king had loved before he became ruler of the
English. This was Edith, surnamed 'Swanneshals', which in the
vernacular means 'Swan-neck'. She had at one time been the
king's concubine,[1] and knew the secret marks on the king's body
better than others did, for she had been admitted to a greater
intimacy of his person. Thus they would be assured by her knowledge of his secret marks when they could not be sure from his
external appearance. The reason for this was that, when the mortal
blow was struck, whatever royal insignia he wore were immediately
carried off to the duke so as to be evidence that the king had been
slain. This was the ancient custom, and is still, I believe, modern
practice, that when kings are captured or their fortresses taken,
those who are the first to strip off the king's helmet and offer it to
their king, or who are the first to take the king's standard when a
fortress is captured (especially when the keep of an important
castle is taken) are given large rewards.

When Osgod had brought the woman she pointed out the
king's body amongst the heaps of dead from several identifying
marks. The body was placed by the brethren themselves upon a
bier, and many of the company of Norman warriors paid their
respects to the body all the way to Battlebridge,[2] as it is now called,
and so did a large number of Englishmen who had heard of the
imminent defeat of their men and had caught them up, because the
English had never experienced fellowship with the Normans
before. They brought the body to Waltham and buried it with great
honour, where, without any doubt, he has lain at rest until the

fabulentur homines quod in rupe manserit Dorobernie et nuper defunctus sepultus sit Cestrie,[1] pro certo quiescit Walthamie: cuius corporis translatione, quoniam sic se habebat status ecclesie fabricandi,[2] uel deuotio fratrum reuerentiam corpori exibentium,[3] nunc extreme memini me tertio affuisse et, sicut uulgo celebre est et attestationes antiquorum audiuimus, plagas ipsis ossibus impressas oculis corporeis et uidisse et manibus contrectasse.

fo. 106ʳ   Vixit | autem et Anglis imperauit egregius rex iste modico tempore per annum et ⟨∗∗∗⟩[a] menses[4] et uiam uniuerse carnis ingressus appositus est ad patres suos.

xxii. *Qualiter post mortem regis Willelmi successit Willelmus Rufus qui spoliauit ecclesiam de Waltham.*

Deinde dux ille nobilis[b] consecratus in regem iura regnorum Anglis instituit, et consuetudines e diuersis regnorum partibus, quas decentiores et nobilibus uiris aptiores inuestigare potuit, regno suo instituit,[5] ita quod nobiles terre sue generosorum filios regum curiis et minorum etiam terris presidentium exploratores[c] nobilium consuetudinum et facesciarum applicaret;[6] nichil tamen derogans predecessorum suorum traditionibus honestis, scilicet regum Anglicorum, a quibus se gaudeant Normanni reges nostri quod precipuum est in omni munificentia et regni gloria et morum honestate et corporis habitudine decenti suscepisse.

fo. 106ᵛ   Multos | rex iste complens dies, in senectute bona consummatus, expleuit tempora multa et ipse appositus est ad patres suos, regni sui uicesimo secundo anno. Successit ei filius Willelmus, Ruphus cognomento, heres quidem benefitiorum set degener morum, cui breues annos credimus indultos quia concessis sibi

---

ᵃ *lacuna C*; et menses *H*   ᵇ nobilis ille *H*   ᶜ exploranteres *C*

---

[1] For later legends about Harold's burial place, see above, pp. xliv–xlv.
[2] Building work or restoration was being carried out in the 1120s; see Fernie, 'Romanesque church', p. 73.
[3] See above, pp. xiii, xiv, xlv–xlvi, for the care taken by the canons to avoid the growth of a cult at Harold's tomb.
[4] There is a lacuna in both the Cotton and the Harleian MSS, so the number may never have been added in the original. However, Harold reigned for little more than ten months, from 6 January until 14 October; this is another indication of the author's hazy knowledge of the chronology of the 11th cent.
[5] Taken literally, this passage seems to imply the mixture of old customs (varying in different kingdoms), pre-Conquest law codes, and new customs that did in fact exist in 12th-cent. England, and led to such compilations as the *Leges Henrici Primi*. Although

present day, whatever stories men may invent that Harold dwelt in a cave at Canterbury and that later, when he died, was buried at Chester.[1] I can now in my old age remember that I was present when his body was translated for the third time, occasioned either by the state of building work in the church[2] or because the brethren out of devotion were showing reverence for the body.[3] It is generally well-known, and we have heard men of old testify, that men saw with their own eyes, and touched with their hands, the marks of the wounds visible on the very bones. But his life had ended, and that noble king, having ruled the English for a short time only of a year and ⟨some⟩ months,[4] went the way of all flesh and was gathered unto his fathers.

22. After the death of King William he was succeeded by William Rufus who pillaged the church of Waltham.

After the noble duke was crowned king he established for the English the laws of his predecessors and such customs as he could discover from different parts of the kingdoms that were more honourable and fitting for men of noble rank.[5] So he attached to the courts of kings, and even to lesser rulers of lands, the sons of noblemen from his own land to learn about the customs of good lordship befitting men of rank;[6] yet this in no way detracted from the honourable traditions of his predecessors, the English kings, from whom our Norman kings should rejoice that they have inherited all that is best in the English spirit of generosity, in their pride in their kingdom, in their virtuous way of life and in their fine physical strength.

After a rule of many years the king died at a good old age and, having lived a full and active life, he was gathered unto his fathers in the twenty-second year of his reign. His son William, called Rufus, succeeded him and inherited his estates, but he was a man of bad character, and we believe he was granted only a few years

the Chronicler may not have been consciously aware of the legal and customary complexities, he may have had some knowledge, however vague, of the different elements in the changes he and older men he knew had experienced.

[6] It was becoming normal practice in north-western Europe during the 11th cent. for the sons of men of rank to be sent to the courts of kings or counts to be brought up and trained as knights. The education of boys usually began about the age of seven, but mature men were attracted to renowned courts; see M. Chibnall, *The World of Orderic Vitalis* (Oxford, 1984), pp. 119–21, 132–3; Barlow, *William Rufus*, pp. 14–25.

benefitiis a domino minus aptus nec ecclesie deuotus sicut expediret, nec iusticie strenuus executor set 'uir desideriorum'[1]
eisque indulgens semper extitit. In tantam igitur uesaniam ad
cumulum et exaggerationem miserie sue ausus prorumpere ut
ecclesiam Walthamensem, a deuotis patribus predictis tam sanctis
desideriis, tam deuotis multarum opulentiarum benefitiis, ornatam et Dei munimine fundatam inuadere, et nullo respectu habito

fo. 107ʳ sanctorum patrocinatus ecclesie presidentium uel re|uerentia
predecessorum eam instituentium, spoliare et omnia ipsius benefitia diripere predonis more non dubitaret, uilia censens Anglorum
instituta nec eo usque ualitura quin eis eligeret ditare predecessorum sepulturas[a] et ecclesiam Cadomensem ex rapina ornare, et
spoliis Walthamensis ecclesie salubre remedium credens animarum patris et matris ibi quiescentium si de alieno et quasi ab
uno altari distracto aliud ornetur et quasi munus gratum et ualde
pretiosum alicui patri offerantur precisa proprii membra filii.

Sicut enim in scripto inuenimus autentico manibus ipsius
magistri Adelardi qui tunc preerat ecclesie exarato, sex milibus et
sexcentis et sexaginta sex libris[2] appensum est quod una uice tulit

fo. 107ᵛ ab ecclesia in capsis aureis et argenteis, in crucibus, textis, | et aliis
ornamentis aureis et argenteis; ipsam etiam casulam auro textam
que uocata est 'Dominus dixit ad me' quam supra memorauimus;[3]
quatuor etiam campanas illius temporis pretiosas, et thesaurum
inestimabilem quo instaurauit duas ecclesias Cadomi, ecclesiam[b]
scilicet Sancti Stephani quam fundauit pater eius, et ecclesiam[c]
Sancte Trinitatis quam fundauit mater eius,[4] que scilicet usque
hodie spoliis gaudent sic adquisitis et inscripta habent nomina in
ipsis capsis et textis principum qui ea contulerunt ecclesie Walthamensi testimonio et auctoritate archiepiscopi Ginsi.

Compunctus igitur corde rex ille diuino nutu quod tantam

---

[a] sepultura C   [b] ecclesiam suam H   [c] ecclesiam suam H

---

[1] The phrase comes from Daniel, 10: 11, but is there used in a different sense (of *good*
passions).
[2] This figure, roughly two-thirds of 10,000, is equivalent to 10,000 marks of silver and
is evidently a round figure rather than an exact valuation.
[3] See above, cap. 16.
[4] Some of the treasures that William Rufus took from churches were used to finance
a loan to his crusading brother, Robert Curthose (Orderic, v. 208–9). This passage,
however, implies that the spoils of Waltham went (or were believed to have gone) to
enrich the churches at Caen. A charter of Rufus for St Stephen's, Caen, grants some
lands in England in exchange for the regalia which his father had bequeathed to the

because he was not fit to enjoy the benefits bestowed on him by the Lord; he was neither devoted to the service of the church, nor did he administer justice vigorously, but he was a 'man of passions'[1] which he always indulged. The result was that he was rash enough to break out into such acts of madness as to heap up trouble for himself. The church of Waltham had been adorned by those devout ancestors we have mentioned with rich gifts, given in a spirit of pious devotion, and the church had been founded under God's protection. Yet he did not hesitate to assail it, pillage it, and plunder all its ornaments like a robber, with no regard for the saints who watch over and protect the church, and no respect for his predecessors who had established it. He considered the institutions of the English contemptible and of no worth except to make use of them to enrich the tombs of his ancestors, and to adorn the church of Caen from the plunder. He believed that the spoils of Waltham church would provide sure salvation for the souls of his father and mother lying at rest at Caen, if the altar there were adorned from the other altar at Waltham, dismembered as it were. It was as though the limbs of one's own true son were being cut off and offered as an acceptable and very precious gift to someone else's father.

We have discovered from an authentic document written in the hand of Master Adelard himself, who was at that time in charge of the church, that the weight of the things removed from the church on the one occasion amounted to 6,666 pounds,[2] consisting of gold and silver reliquaries, crosses, gospel books, and other gold and silver ornaments. Amongst these was the very chasuble woven in gold which we mentioned previously,[3] called 'The Lord Spake Unto Me'. There were also four valuable bells of that time and a priceless treasure which he used to restore the two churches of Caen, namely, the church of St Stephen, which his father had founded, and the church of the Holy Trinity founded by his mother.[4] Even to this day they rejoice in the spoils thus acquired, and have inscriptions on the very reliquaries and gospel books of the names of the leading men who, on the testimony and authority of Archbishop Cynesige, bestowed them upon the church of Waltham.

However, pricked in his conscience by divine will for having so

abbey, and it is possible that he also gave some treasures not recorded in the charter (Lucien Musset, *Les Actes de Guillaume le Conquérant et de la reine Mathilde pour les abbayes caennaises* (Mémoires de la Société des Antiquaires de Normandie, xxvii, 1967), no. 24).

ecclesie iniuriam commisit,[a] penitentia ductus, uillam Walthamensem cum omnibus ei adiacentibus ad resarcianda dampna
fo. 108ʳ prescripta eidem ecclesie | perpetuo mansuram dedit, et scripto[1]
confirmauit post mortem Walcherii Dunelmensis episcopi cui
dederat eam pater suus illustris ille rex Willelmus ut haberet ibi
domicilium cum uocaretur a remotis ubi habitabat[2] partibus ad
consilium,[b] nam in conquisitione terre istius adduxerat eum rex
secum, uirum prudentem, litteratum, et in consiliis dandis regno
utilibus ualde discretum.[3]

xxiii. Qui dederunt Waltham ecclesie nostre.

Auctores donationis uille Walthamensis laudamus: Toui le Prude
qui primus eam instituit de noualibus et, auctore Cnuto et eius filio
Hardecnuto, fecit eam confirmari sub anathematis uinculo. Laudamus etiam presentem hunc Willelmum qui ob reconciliandam
sibi crucifixi gratiam quam offendisse plurimum non dubitamus in
fo. 108ᵛ huius perpetratione spoliationis, qui | eam carta sua[4] ecclesie con-
firmauit et, sub predicto anathematis edicto, assistentibus archi-
episcopis, episcopis, et uniuerso clero, communiter roborauit.
Caueant sibi successores et memores conditionis sue sibi reser-
uent que sunt Cesaris, et soluant que sunt Dei Deo,[5] ne lacessitus
et sepenumero[c] ad iram prouocatus inducat maledictionem pro
benedictione, et sint 'nouissima hominis illius peiora prioribus'.[6]

xxiiii. Qualiter furata erant uasa aurea.

Dignum igitur duximus transire ad miracula que quidem oculis
fidelibus uidere meruimus, uel a uiris autenticis illius temporis

---

[a] om. C   [b] concilium C   [c] sine numero usque H

---

[1] This charter has not survived; the only document from the reign of Rufus preserved
in the Waltham cartularies is a writ instructing his sheriffs to allow the canons to have
their lands and customs as in his father's time (Ransford, *Waltham Charters*, no. 2).

[2] William the Conqueror gave Waltham and some other lands to Walcher bishop of
Durham (SD i. 113–14), who was murdered in 1080; the restoration of part of the former
endowment in his son's reign was probably made either in 1091, when Walcher's
successor William of Saint-Calais was exiled after a celebrated trial, or in 1096 when he
died. The author apparently confuses the two bishops, and the restoration cannot have
been entirely effective, since Queen Matilda later restored 2½ hides of Northland in
Waltham unjustly taken away by Walcher (Ransford, *Waltham Charters*, no. 10).

greatly wronged the church and brought to repentance, the king gave to the same church to hold in perpetuity the vill of Waltham, with all the lands attached to it, so that the aforesaid losses suffered by it might be made good. He confirmed this in a written document[1] after the death of Walcher, bishop of Durham, to whom his father, the noble King William, had given it so that the bishop might have a house there when he was called from the distant regions where he lived[2] to give counsel, for the king had brought him with him when he had conquered the land as he was a man of knowledge and letters, and very discerning in the counsel he gave which was beneficial to the realm.[3]

23. *Those who gave Waltham to our church.*

We praise those who were responsible for the gift of the vill of Waltham: Tovi the Proud, who was the first to found it from newly-tilled lands, and then, on the authority of Cnut and his son Harthacnut, had it confirmed under a binding anathema. We also praise this same William who, to regain the favour of the Crucified One, whom we do not doubt he had greatly offended when he committed his acts of plunder, confirmed his endowment upon the church with his own charter.[4] Under the proclamation of the above-mentioned anathema, and in the presence of the archbishops, bishops, and the whole of the clergy, he publicly confirmed it. Let his successors take warning and, mindful of their condition, let them keep the things that are Caesar's and render to God the things which are God's[5] lest, being provoked and frequently angered, he bring upon them a curse instead of a blessing, and 'the last state of that man be worse than the first'.[6]

24. *The theft of the golden vessels.*

I have thought it right now to pass on to the miracles which we were privileged to see with our believing eyes, or which we learned from men of authority living at that time had taken place,

---

[3] Walcher was a learned secular priest from Lotharingia; see Barlow, *The English Church 1066–1154* (London, 1979), p. 62.

[4] See above, n. 1.

[5] Cf. Matt. 22: 21.

[6] Matt. 12: 45.

facta cognouimus, ne uilescant non audita que in oculis Iesu Christi celebria credimus et multa laude digna.

Scriptum legimus quod in primitiua huius ecclesie institutione fo. 109ʳ quatuor | sub furua nocte inimici crucis Christi[a] subfodientes ecclesias[1] ornamenta quedam ecclesie furati sunt, uasa quidem opere fusili ex argento fabricata; que transferre cupientes ad loca non sancta, cecitate cordis necnon et oculorum eo usque obducti sunt ut itinerandi quo disposuerant negaretur eis ex toto facultas, et per totam noctem per deuia et loca aquosa,[2] querentes requiem et non inuenientes, euagarentur. Mane facto, ducatu cuiusdam uiatoris uix perducti sunt Lundoniam[b] in cuius introitu forte fortuitu obuiam habuerunt quendam nomine Theodoricum, in opere fusili auri et argenti totius ciuitatis precipuum,[3] qui et ipse manibus suis ista fabrefecerat; cui exponentes merces suas et quanto eas emere uellet requirentes respondit se cito reuersurum fo. 109ᵛ et in domo sua de precio | et precii solutione satisfacturum.

Diuertens interea uir ille discretus et sagax huiusce operum, memor etiam quod hec fabricasset ad opus ecclesie Walthamensis ad nutum et uoluntatem nobilis illius matrone Glithe uxoris Toui le Prude,[4] conuocatis secum quibusdam uicinis, cum conuenisset de precio expositarum mercium, 'Fures estis', inquid, 'et latrones; thesaurum ecclesie Walthamensis furtiue diripuistis, nam et hec eadem uasa manibus meis operata et ecclesie Walthamensi collata per ingenuam matronam Glitham, omni dubietate semota, horum uicinorum meorum testimonio, non ambigimus. Cum omni[c] igitur festinantia furtiua hec reportabitis ad loca sancta, adiunctis uobis de ciuitate hac uiris prudentibus in quorum presentia pro meritis fo. 110ʳ suscipietis commissi talionem, | et dignas reatus uestri penas secundum terre consuetudinem exsoluetis.' Quod ita factum esʈ.

ᵃ *om. H*   ᵇ *Lond' H*   ᶜ *om. H*

---

[1] The author occasionally uses the plural where the singular might be expected, a practice possibly derived from the Latin poets (see above, p. xxx). Sometimes, as here, the practice causes ambiguity; the meaning may be that the thieves were robbing a number of churches, including Waltham. If taken literally, *subfodientes ecclesias* would suggest that they dug under the walls, which would have been more likely if the churches were made of timber (cf. Fernie, 'Romanesque church', pp. 50, 75 n. 8). However, recent excavations have shown the existence of one or two pre-Conquest stone churches at Waltham, so perhaps the passage should not be taken too literally when applied to the church here. For the whole episode, see above, pp. xxxvi–xxxvii.

[2] Cf. Luke 11:24, where the clause 'perambulat per loca inaquosa, quaerens requiem et non inueniens' is applied to an unclean spirit; here the *loca inaquosa* through which he wandered are changed, appropriately for the Essex marshes, to *loca aquosa*.

so that those things which I believe are honourable in the sight of Jesus Christ and are worthy of much praise should not lose their importance through not being heard.

I have seen it written that during the original founding of this church four enemies of the Cross of Christ, tunnelling beneath the church[1] one dark night, stole certain ornaments belonging to it, vessels made of cast silver. They wanted to transfer them to unconsecrated places, but they were so blinded in heart as well as sight that they were utterly prevented from travelling to their intended destination. Throughout the whole of the night they wandered about over trackless, marshy places,[2] seeking rest but finding none. When it was morning they reached London, but only with difficulty and guided by a certain traveller. On their entry to the city they happened to meet a man named Theodoric who was the finest craftsman in the city in cast gold and silver work.[3] It was he himself who had made these articles with his own hands. When they displayed their merchandise and asked him how much he was willing to pay for those things he replied that he would shortly return and in his own house meet their demands over the price and its payment.

Meanwhile that prudent man, who was an expert in such works of art, parted from them. He remembered that he had made these articles for use in the church at Waltham at the wish and command of the noble lady Gytha, wife of Tovi the Proud.[4] He therefore called together some neighbours, and agreement was reached on the price of the merchandise set before them. 'You', he said, 'are thieves and robbers; you have cunningly plundered the treasure of Waltham church, for I made these vessels with my own hands and they were presented to the church by the noble lady Gytha. We are in no doubt at all and are not mistaken about this, and these neighbours of mine are witnesses to the fact. You will, therefore, with all haste return these articles which you have stolen to that holy place. These good men from the city will join you, and in their presence you will submit to the punishment you deserve for the crime you have committed, paying the proper penalty for your offence in accordance with the custom of the land.' And that is what happened.

[3] Theodoric was goldsmith to Edward the Confessor and William the Conqueror; he held five estates in Berkshire and ministerial estates to the south of Southwark in 1066 (*DB* i. 36, 63); see Freeman, *Norman Conquest*, iv. 41.

[4] See above, cap. 13.

Nam primus, qui se clericum confessus est, candenti ferro clauis ecclesie in facie signatus est. Reliqui capitalem subiere sententiam, et ecclesie Dei[a] restitutum est quod suum erat.

Multa et illius temporis miracula in scriptum non sunt redacta, tum penuria scriptorum, tum segnium socordia qui tunc aderant prelatorum,[1] gens enim tunc sancta et modernorum respectu immaculata pro facili ducebant talia. Signa enim infidelibus, non fidelibus, data sunt; uacillaret nanque ad presens tenuis fides nostra, nisi nouis morbis nostris superuenientibus quandoque miraculis, noua accederent remedia. Exemplum placeat. Dedu-

fo. 110ᵛ catur in medium beatus ille Thomas, | extremus quidem martirum[b] in Anglia,[2] set inter precipuos primitiuorum conputandus; deducatur in medium status ecclesie ante passionem eius qualis fuerit apud nos, quid postea contulerit regno mors sancti uiri,[3] et propter illum Dei miseratio et manifeste quis poterit agnoscere non inania fuisse miracula[4] que fidem pene omnium extenuatam et plus solito uacillantem reduxerunt ad gratiam, ut ubi diffusius habundauerat peccatum, superhabundaret et gratia.[5] Vigebat enim necessitas ut meritis sancti martiris grauiorem dominus in seruis suis peccatorum languorem curando quante sit benignitatis in filios manifestaret, et incrementis crebrescentibus miserationum suarum fecundaretur ecclesia que iam pene in exterminium, peccatis

fo. 111ʳ nostris | exigentibus, erat deuoluta.

xxv. *Quam ordinate se habebant canonici in primis.*

Puer ego quinque annorum (uidi usque ad presentia tempora multa) canonicus[6] constitutus in ecclesia Sancte Crucis a bone memorie Ernulpho decano, assensu et donatione uenerabilis domine Adeliza regine,[7] cuius tunc donationis erant prebende, et

---

ᵃ *om. H*   ᵇ *lacuna* mar . . . *H*

[1] It is not clear whether the author is referring to stories of miracles which took place in the church at Waltham or in the wider church; if to the former, then he must be speaking of a time when no particularly strong rule governed the life of the clergy, perhaps before Adelard's arrival.

[2] A reference to the murder of Becket on 29 December 1170; he was canonized by Pope Alexander III on 21 February 1173 (see Frank Barlow, *Thomas Becket* (London, 1986), pp. 268–9; Raymonde Foreville, 'Canterbury et la canonisation des saints au xiie siècle', *Tradition and Change*, ed. Diana Greenway *et al.* (Cambridge, 1985), pp. 69–70).

[3] This may possibly be an oblique, but generous, allusion to the new foundations established by Henry II in expiation of Becket's murder.

[4] The miracles alleged to have taken place at his tomb were decisive in persuading

The first of them, who confessed to being a clerk, was branded on the face with the red-hot iron of the church key. The others were sentenced to death, and the property of God's church was restored to it.

There were many miracles of that time which were not recorded both because of a lack of scribes and also because of the negligence and inactivity of contemporary prelates;[1] indeed, the people of those days, being holy and pure-hearted compared with modern people, took such miracles for granted. In fact, it was to non-believers that signs were given rather than to believers, whereas today our weak faith would be wavering were it not for the recent succour we have received in the miracles which have come at last to save us from our latest ills. For example, consider the blessed Thomas, the most recent of martyrs in England,[2] who must be considered among the foremost of our archbishops; then consider the condition of our Church as it had been in the time before Thomas' martyrdom and what the death of this holy man later bestowed upon the realm.[3] It was because of him that we received God's mercy and the faculty to recognize clearly that the miracles[4] were not in vain which restored to grace the faith which, in the case of almost all of us, had grown weak and more than usually frail, so that where sin abounded grace might much more abound.[5] There was a great need for the Lord to heal, through the merits of the holy martyr, the serious sickness in His servants resulting from their sins, so that He might reveal how great is His kindness towards His children, and the Church be greatly enriched by His many mercies, a Church which had now been almost consigned to destruction because of the weight of our sins.

25. *In their early years the canons lived according to a rule.*

As a boy of five—I have seen much happen since then—I was received as a canon[6] of the church of the Holy Cross by Dean Arnulf of happy memory by assent and gift of the venerable lady Queen Adeliza,[7] the prebends being at that time in her gift. My

Pope Alexander III to accept the popular demand for Becket's canonization (see *Materials*, vii. 531–3, 544–5).   [5] Cf. Rom. 5: 20.

[6] See above, cap. 11, where he speaks of his fifty-three years in the church at Waltham; he must therefore have been fifty-eight when he was expelled from the church with the other secular canons in 1177.

[7] For Waltham as queen's dower, see above, p. xxvii; for her charters to Waltham, see Ransford, *Waltham Charters*, nos. 16, 17, 18.

ad prima litterarum rudimenta traditus magistro Petro, filio magistri Athelardi institutoris et ordinatoris presentis ecclesie.[1] Fons enim uberrimus disciplinis doctrine tunc scaturiebat ab ipso Petro secundum modum Teutonicorum, non enim obstantibus lectionibus uel litteris et uersibus componendis minus addiscebatur et frequentabatur in ecclesia cantus. Et ordinatissima

fo. 111ᵛ distinctio puerilis habitudinis ita ut, more religiosorum | fratrum, honeste et non sine grauitate incederent, starent, legerent, et cantarent, et quicquid ad gradum chori*a* uel in ipso choro cantare oportebat, corde tenus unus uel duo, uel plures, absque libri solatio cantarent et psallerent. In choro constituti, non respiciebat puer alterum, nisi forte ex obliquo tamen raro, nec faceret ei uerbum unum; non discurrebant per chorum nisi quibus fuisset iniunctum a magistro pro cappis aut pro libris transferendis uel aliis quibuslibet causis; manentes in choro, sicut processione procedentes, a scolis intrant chorum sic exeuntes intrant scolas ad modum canonicorum de nocte surgentium.[2]

xxvi. *Qualiter mulier, furando denarium super altare, contracta est omnibus diebus uite sue.*

fo. 112ʳ Tempore igitur Resurrectionis quod celebriter agebatur in ecclesia nostra a Pascha usque Pentecosten, die quadam Sabbati, psallentibus in choro fratribus festiue in uesperis ut assolent illis temporibus, mulier e uicino de Enefelde, deuotionis intuitu, accedens ad altare sancte crucis denarium optulit; post oblationem statim recessit. Erat et in ipso pago nostro mulier paupercula hostiatim mendicans panem, certe amaro satis animo nec minus uerbo, Editha Crikel[3] dicta, ex re nomen trahens quoniam titubando incedebat duobus baculis, hinc inde fulta; hec accessit ad altare ut offerret sicut uisum erat nobis, et nummum quem antea deposuerat fidelis illa matrona lambens lingua ab altari furtiue asportauit; set iniuriarum ultrix manus non abfuit, descendenti |

fo. 112ᵛ enim a tertio gradu altaris pars corporis a renibus supra sic distorta

---

a cori C

---

[1] See above, p. xxxi.
[2] Cf. *Reg. Chrod.*, caps. 12, 24, 46.
[3] *Cricce* is the Old English word for 'crutch' or 'staff'.

early education was entrusted to Master Peter, the son of Master Adelard, the first teacher and regulator of the present church.[1]

Indeed a rich spring of instruction in the disciplines flowed from Peter himself in accordance with the methods of the Germans, for the study and reading of Latin and the composition of verses did not prevent singing being learnt and constantly practised in the church. The mien of the boys was so strictly controlled that, like their 'regular' brethren, they would walk, stand, read, and sing in a becoming and dignified manner, and whatever they had to sing on the step of the choir, or in the choir itself, one or two boys, or more, would sing or chant by heart without the help of a book. Once in his place in the choir one boy did not look at another unless, perhaps, askance, and then rarely, nor did he utter a single word to him. The boys did not run through the choir unless they had been ordered to do so by the master for the purpose of transferring copes or books, or for some other reason. They remained in the choir in the order they walked in procession, and as they entered the choir from the schools so they entered the schools when leaving the choir, like canons rising in the night.[2]

26. *A woman was deformed for the rest of her life through stealing a penny which was on the altar.*

It was the season of Easter, which in our church was celebrated from Easter Sunday until Pentecost. One Saturday when the brethren were singing psalms with festal celebration in the choir at Vespers, as they are accustomed to do on those occasions, a woman from nearby Enfield went up to the altar of the holy cross in the course of her worship and made an offering of a penny. After doing this she immediately returned to her place. There was also in that district of ours a poor woman who begged for her bread from house to house, as sharp-tongued indeed as she was ill-natured. She was called Edith Crickel,[3] taking her name from the fact that she walked falteringly on two sticks, supporting herself first on the one and then on the other. This woman approached the altar to make an offering, or so we thought, but the coin which the devout lady previously laid there she licked up with her tongue and craftily carried off from the altar. However, the hand that punishes wrongdoings was not wanting, for as she descended from the third step of the altar her body became so deformed from the waist up

est ut toto tempore uite pars anterior celum supina respiceret, et anus tremula, nunquam compos sui effecta, sic extremum diem clauderet.

Quibus autem inditiis furtiuum hoc claruerit astantium oculis audiatur. Sicut supra memoratum est, descendens a nouissimo gradu miserabilis illa mulier cepit se male habere nauseanti similis et quasi in gutture aliquid haberet inpedimenti unde statim suffocari deberet, capud intermisse excutiens, spumas ore habundanter emittens: quod uidens quidam custos ecclesie Antonius[1] nomine accessit et sicut ille magnus erat et grandis stature trino ictu immani inter scapulas mulieris eiecit ab ore eius coagulum sanguinis ad instar pomi. Cui exanimi et pre angustia uerbi *fo. 113ʳ* palpitanti, prius | accurrerunt qui in presbiterio astabant laici, et cum cognouissent causam ex ore mulieris tante miserie, accurrentes dum cantaretur ymnus 'Ad cenam agni prouidi'[2] ad dominum Brienum Bainard, seniorem tunc et precipuum omnium nostrorum, qui et ipse sacerdos uesperas cantabat, narrauerunt ex ordine que contigerant; quorum uerbis fidem habens, et maxime illius nostri Antonii sacriste, imposita ei ab archichoro antiphona ad 'Magnificat', exultans uir bonus et prudens incepit 'Te Deum laudamus' quod quidem in iubilo decantatum est, et pulsato classico non sine multa lacrimarum plebis ubertate laudantium Dominum qui, in crucis commendandam memorabilem excellentiam, operatus sit hec magnalia successoribus monimenta.

fo. 113ᵛ Psallentibus fratribus, Antonius | ecclesie custos manu propria eiicere uolens sanguinem, immo ut uerum dicam, saniem quam oculis uidi accurrens puer cum pueris nescius talium, expressit nummum, set post uesperas delatus ad presentiam omnium nummus patefecit archana. Nam confessio eis fatue mulieris furtum pandit, et furti causam gemendo coram multis obtexit hanc ita se habentem, corpore distorto uidelicet toto tempore uite sue.

---

[1] See above, p. xxxii.
[2] A 5th-cent. hymn used for Vespers at Eastertide; see *EEFL*, no. 698, p. 452.

that for the rest of her life the front of her body was bent back and she looked skywards. The old woman, who was trembling, never again had control of herself, and that was how she was up to the end of her life.

Let it be understood that it was because of these signs that this theft was revealed to the eyes of the bystanders. As has just been related, the wretched woman began to be ill as she reached the last step, and appeared to be vomiting, as though she had something stuck in her throat which would soon choke her, but she tossed her head continually, and frothed greatly at the mouth. Seeing this a custodian of the church, called Anthony,[1] who was tall and of large stature, went up to her and, striking the woman three mighty blows between her shoulders, made her cough up a clot of blood the size of an apple. As she was out of breath and was panting in a difficult attempt to speak, the people who were standing in the presbytery at first ran to her and, when they learned from what the woman said why she was in such distress, they ran to Dom Brian Baynard while the hymn *Ad cenam agni prouidi*[2] was being sung. He was then the senior in status and in charge of us all, and as a priest was himself singing Vespers. They related to him the details of what had happened. He believed what they told him, especially what Anthony the sacristan had said and, though the choirmaster had directed him to sing the antiphon to the 'Magnificat', this good and wise man began with joy the 'Te Deum laudamus', which was sung with jubilation; and when the bells rang out the people, weeping copious tears, praised the Lord who had wrought these great things as a memorial for posterity, so that they might honour the extraordinary power of the Cross.

As the brethren sang psalms, Anthony, the custodian of the church, wishing to disperse the blood, or rather the bloody matter, with his own hands (indeed, to tell the truth, I saw this with my own eyes when, as a boy, I was hurrying along with the other boys, though I did not understand what was happening), then extracted the coin. After Vespers the coin was brought into the presence of all of us, and the mystery explained. For the confession of the foolish woman revealed her theft to them, and by complaining about the reason for the theft in front of many people she hid from them her condition, I mean that her body was deformed for the whole of her life.

xxvii. *Qualiter quidam percussus est igne infernali et sanatus per sanctam crucem.*

Ad laudem igitur et gloriam sancte crucis, quod oculis uidimus, quibus interesse miseratione diuina meruimus, posterorum mentibus imprimenda uera assertione decreuimus. Erat in pago Walthamensi clericus, Crispinus nomine, prebendulam habens fo. 114ʳ modicam, nullam quidem | de predictis .xii. set unam de duabus quas de cibariis suis canonici sibi constituerant clericis qui ewangelium uicissim legerent in missis capitularibus,[1] qui etiam ad negotia ecclesie ordinanda uel transmutanda ad uotum capituli mitterentur propriis sumptibus. Hic fratrem habebat nomine Matheum, iuuenem pulcrum, sapientem, satis prudentem, quales creare consueuit*ᵃ* Waltham, quia*ᵇ* de amplis pascuis pratorum ciuitatule nostre pullos bonos, et de indigenis homines ualde strenuos, inde prodeuntes certe sepe uidimus. Matheus iste, sicut Domino placuit, peccatis exigentibus, in ulteriori parte percussus ulcere pessimo pluribus annis uitam duxit non in desideriis et deliciis; pes enim eius dexter, si bene recolo, igne aduerso qui fo. 114ᵛ uulgo Grecus dicitur,[2] miserabiliter accensus iam consump|tus erat usque ad talum. Talus quidem, sicut accepimus a phisicis,[3] cartilaginosus suscipit neruos a superioribus, cuius lesuram, etsi modicam, nature scimus esse et corporis saluti ualde contrariam. E uicino igitur ignis iste infernalis talo propinquans, ut pene nulla esset ipsius distantia, egrotare cepit plus solito et uicibus angustiarum et tortionum crebrescentibus, uite ipsius desperatio cepit mentes propinquorum admodum turbare.

Habebat hic matrem nomine Mabiliam, germanam domini

ᵃ consueuerat *H*   *ᵇ* qd' *late insertion in margin C*; qd' *H*

---

[1] This is evidence of the sub-division of the original prebends to endow new members of the community, in this case two clerks who were performing the duties of lectors.

[2] Crispin was evidently suffering from ergotism, a type of gangrene caused by ergot in rye, and more usually known from the 12th cent. onwards as 'St Anthony's fire'. The Order of the Hospitallers of St Anthony was founded *c.* 1100 and their hospital at La Motte became a pilgrimage centre for sufferers from ergotism (D. H. Farmer, *The Oxford Dictionary of Saints*, 2nd edn. (Oxford, 1987), pp. 22–3). The use of the term 'Greek fire' for this affliction is unusual; it was more usually applied to a combustible composition used to set fire to enemy ships, and occurs in the earliest chronicles of the crusades (see *Gesta Francorum*, NMT, p. 78; Orderic v. 138, citing Baudri of Dol). The term *sacer ignis* occurs in classical writings for conditions ranging from anthrax (Vergil, *Georgics*, iii. 566) to erysipelas (Columella, *De re rustica*, vii. 5. 16, Celsus, *De Medicina*, v. 28. 4) and

27. A man was stricken with a dreadful inflammation and healed through the holy cross.

We have therefore decided that what we have seen with our own eyes and have been privileged to experience by the mercy of God we must, for the praise and glory of the holy cross, impress upon the minds of posterity by declaring the truth. There was in the district of Waltham a clerk named Crispin who had a very small prebend. This was not one of the previously mentioned twelve, but was one of two prebends which the canons had established from their own food-allowances for clerks who were to take turns at reading the Gospel at chapter masses,[1] and who, at the bidding of the chapter, and at their own expense, were to be commissioned to organize or change the affairs of the church. This Crispin had a brother called Matthew, a handsome young man who was wise and very intelligent, one of the kind of men that Waltham used to produce. Certainly in those days we frequently saw fine young men come like colts from the ample pasture of the meadows of our small town, very strong men of native stock. This Matthew, for so it pleased God, his sins weighing heavily upon him, lived for many years without pleasure or enjoyment, suffering severely from a painful ulcer. His right foot, if I recollect rightly, was badly inflamed and affected right up to the ankle with an inflammation which is commonly called 'Greek fire'.[2] The ankle, we learn from physicians,[3] is full of sinews, and receives these from limbs above it. Any injury to it, however slight, we know is inimical to the natural health of the body. So as that hellish inflammation was reaching the ankle from the foot close by, for the infection was very close to the ankle, it began to grow worse than usual and, as his distress and pain increased in turn, his relatives began to despair for his life and to be very anxious in mind.

His mother was called Mabel, sister of Lord Richard of

shingles (Pliny, *Nat. Hist.*, xxvi. 121); but the Waltham chronicler is unlikely to have known any of these works.

[3] This statement seems to derive ultimately, but very indirectly, from Hippocrates (LCL, iii. 392–4), who discusses injuries to bones and ligaments of the foot, and the danger of mortification of the heel. It is most improbable that a translation of Hippocrates was known in Waltham in the late 12th cent.; but miscellaneous fragments of information derived from older traditions, or perhaps from the works of Constantine the African, may have been included in a medical anthology, perhaps the volume described as *De Phisica* in the library catalogue (M. R. James, 'Manuscripts from Essex monastic libraries', *TEAS*, new ser., xxi (1937), 44).

Ricardi de Hastinges, magistri militie Templi in Anglia,[1] mulierem profecto sanctam, uite probabilis, sancte conuersationis, cuius inter monacas conuictus et coabitatio splendidam eam reddiderunt apud Wikes,[2] usque ad hec nouissima tempora nostra. Cum hec agerentur de quibus mentio | presens dat intellectum auditui,[3] etsi in extremis uideret filium suum laborantem nec aliud nisi instantem mortis horam prestolantem, maluit plus anime prouidere quam uite et, institutis inibi consanguineis et uicinis qui funeralibus obsequiis operam darent, assumptis secum duabus filiabus suis, elegit utilius pro filio et prestantius in ecclesia ante crucifixum lacrimosis suspiriis insistere et orationibus ut spiritus filii iam migraturus ab ergastulo cenulente materie dirigeretur ad Dominum quam sedulis manibus oculos claudere morientis, quod quidem supplicium ydiotarum et uetularum est commune solatium. Vbi cum ab hora conpletorii usque ad medie noctis conticinium, mater pro filio preces funderet (et uere mater que quidem usque ad sanguinem | eliciendum lacrimis non pepercisset), accidit dictu mirabile, credi mirabilius; uecordis enim est animi et insensati credere Deum fidelibus lacrimis et interne deuotionis affectu pro carorum salute non posse moueri, dum singultibus multiplicatis non contineret mater lacrimas, nec contineret misericors ille et dulcis Iesus misericordias suas.[4] Nam qui presto est omnibus inuocantibus eum in ueritate iam, quasi tedio affectus ubertate lacrimarum et singultus, infirmanti presens affuit, nam ymago presens huius crucifixi quam cernere potestis obstipo sic capite,[5] sic redimita auro, gemmis, et huiuscemodi apparatu, in extremis laboranti apparuit, stans ad pedes lecti, distentis brachiis, sicut nunc est, proprio nomine ab extasi euocans Matheum, sciscitans utrum uite melioris statum et mandatorum | Dei plus solito sedulus esse uelit executor, et bonorum uirorum imitator, non eorum ut assueuit peruicax detractator. Cui cum respondisset se pariturum per omnia, quoniam eorum que improperauerat ei mens erat

fo. 115ʳ *(marginal)*

fo. 115ᵛ *(marginal)*

fo. 116ʳ *(marginal)*

---

[1] Richard of Hastings became Master of the Temple in England on 23 January 1155 (B. Lees, *Records of the Templars in England in the Twelfth Century* (London, 1935), p. xlix); he was not Master at the time this incident took place *c.* 1130 when the author was a boy. He witnessed a charter for Wix priory, where his sister became a nun (C. N. L. Brooke, 'Episcopal charters for Wix priory', *Medieval Miscellany for Doris Stenton* (PRS, 1962), p. 46 n. 3). The close connection of his sister and nephew with Waltham may account partly for the author's generous view of Geoffrey de Mandeville; the Templars secured de Mandeville's posthumous release from excommunication and his Christian burial *c.* 1163 in the graveyard of the New Temple church (*Complete Peerage*, v. 116).

Hastings, Master of the Knights Templar in England.[1] She was a truly holy woman whose manner of life was honourable and pious. As a member of the community of nuns at Wix[2] she gained a reputation which has lasted right down to our own times. When these things were happening (which I am relating so that you may understand when you hear them[3]), though she saw her son in the very throes of death and waiting for nothing but the impending moment of death, she preferred to make provision for his soul rather than his life. Arranging for her relatives and neighbours to be at hand to help with the funeral rites, she took her two daughters with her and chose to do what was more beneficial and efficacious for her son, to stand with tears and sighs before the crucifix in the church, and to pray that her son's spirit, now about to depart from the prison of his sinful flesh, might be taken straight to the Lord. This she did rather than close his eyes in death with dutiful hands, the usual consolation of humble folk and elderly matrons. Here the mother poured out her prayers for her son from the hour of Compline until the silent hour of midnight—she was a true mother who went on weeping till she shed drops of blood— when something occurred marvellous to relate and more marvellous to be believed. Only the foolish and deaf to reason can believe that God cannot be moved by the tears of the faithful and the longing of the deeply devout for the salvation of loved ones. The mother could not contain her tears and sobbed continuously, but the God of compassion[4] and sweet Jesus did not withhold their mercy. Indeed, the One who aids all who call upon Him in truth was now at hand to help her in her weakness, as if wearied by her bitter tears and her wailing. The figure of this crucifix, which you can at present see with 'head bowed',[5] wreathed in gold, and bejewelled, appeared before the sick man similarly adorned, standing at the foot of his bed in his extreme distress, and with arms outstretched, as now, called Matthew by his own name out of his swoon. It asked him whether he wished to experience a better life and to carry out with more than usual zeal the commands of God, emulating good men rather than wilfully decrying them as he used to do. He replied that he would be obedient in all things, for he felt

[2] For Wix (Sopwick), see *Monasticon*, iv. 513; Sally Thompson, *Women Religious* (Oxford, 1991), pp. 10, 230, 257; *VCH Essex*, ii. 124.

[3] Cf. Matt. 13: 13–15.

[4] Another possible example of the use of the plural for the singular; see above, p. 62 n. 1.

[5] Cf. Persius, *Sat*. iii. 80.

conscia, 'Adoro te,' inquid, 'fili Dei uiui, pro me misero peccatore passum in cruce pro mei et totius mundi redemptione; salua me in hac hora quem pauisti pane tuo in ecclesia crucis tue ab uberibus matris mee.'

Apprehendens igitur ymago predicta talum infirmantis putridum proiecit ad ultimum domus angulum, et extremam cruris partem, ubi pes compaginatus fuerat sepius manu circumuoluens, cutem nouam in momento eminentie*a* ossis superduxit similem cuti relique, dolorem omnimodum deleuit, salutem plenam corpori restituit, sicque discessit.

xxviii *Qualiter inueniunt talum exustum in angulo domus.*

fo. 116ᵛ Exultans itaque gaudio ineffabili miser ille misericordiam consecutus, uocat circumiacentes, nam omnes obdormierant, et quid gratie quidue solatii prestitum sit ei per uirtutem sancte crucis cum lacrimis manifestat; cum omni festinantia id matri et sororibus intimari postulat, clerum et populum inuitari ad gratiarum actiones exsoluendas supplex orat.

Nec mora citus euolat nuntius, set uelocior eo campana inuitans ad matutinas[1] sonat; ad ianuam ecclesie sedulus pulsat nec auditur propter eris sonitum donec completur. Accedit sacrista mirans tunsionis tante frequentiam, audit, gaudet, flens gratias agit, sonitum omnium campanarum replicat,[2] ut solet propter ignem in burgo[3] accensum, ut citius conuocaretur clerus et populus ad

fo. 117ʳ miraculum: accedunt canonici, forma|tur processio, accensis cereis et multis luminaribus peruenimus ad domum.

Sciscitantur maiores nostri rei euentus; narrat ille cui fides habenda erat quod acciderat, ueri euentus signa uidimus: ad extremum domus angulum accedimus, ibi sacculum plenum sanie ut uix propter fetorem propinquare quis posset inuenimus;

---

a eminentis *H*

[1] The canons appear to have been sleeping between nocturns and mattins; this would not have been permitted in the original *Regula* (cap. XIII).

[2] Canons and monks were summoned to the offices in the church by the ringing of bells; bells were also rung to announce good news or to warn of danger. For another example of their use to announce a miracle, see *Liber Eliensis*, ed. E. O. Blake (Camden 3rd ser., 1962), p. 299, when Henry I's queen, Matilda, was told in London of the miraculous release of Bricstan from prison through the intervention of St Etheldreda: 'iubet per omnia civitatis monasteria signa pulsari et ab omni ecclesiastici ordinis conventu laudes Deo decantari.'

guilty about the things he had done wrong, and said, 'I worship you, O Son of the living God, for you suffered on the cross for me, a wretched sinner, for my redemption and for that of the whole world. Save me in this hour whom you have fed from my mother's breast with your bread in this church of your Cross.'

This figure then grasping the infected ankle of the sick man, hurled it to the furthest corner of the house, and constantly massaged the end of the leg where the foot had been connected. The bone that jutted out was in an instant covered with new skin like the rest of his skin, and was rid of all pain. His body was fully restored to health, and the figure departed.

28. *They find the inflamed ankle in a corner of the house.*

The poor fellow, having obtained mercy, rejoiced with unspeakable joy, and called those who were lying around him, for all of them had fallen asleep. In tears he showed them what favour and comfort was bestowed upon him through the power of the holy cross. He demanded that the news be taken with all haste to his mother and sisters, and humbly requested that the clergy and people be summoned so that thanksgiving could be expressed.

Without delay a messenger made off in haste, but more swiftly than he, the bell rang summoning the people to Mattins.[1] He beat eagerly upon the door but was not heard for the ringing of the brazen bell till it ceased. The sacristan, amazed at such persistent, loud knocking, came to the door; he heard, he rejoiced, in tears he gave thanks, he renewed the ringing of all the bells[2]—a practice when fire has broken out in the borough[3]—so that the clergy and the people might be summoned more quickly to see the miracle. The canons arrived, a procession was formed, candles were lit, and by the light of many lamps we reached the house.

Our seniors asked for the details of what had happened, and he whom we could not but believe told what had occurred. We saw the evidence of what had truly taken place: we made our way to the furthest corner of the house, found a small bag of pus which scarcely anyone could approach for the stench, and returned

---

[3] The use of the term *burgus* indicates the growth of the settlement in the former vill of Waltham that resulted from the establishment of the collegiate church. The development was in some ways parallel to that of the town of Battle after the founding of the abbey (cf. Eleanor Searle, '*Inter amicos*; the abbey, town and early charters of Battle', *ANS* xiii (1990), 1–3 and n. 3.

gaudentes supra modum reuertimur. Ego quidem tunc puer[1] tur-
ribuli ebdomadarius cum ceteris[2] quandoque flebam, interdum
ridebam, imitatrix simia factus aliorum.

Cum peruentum fuisset ad ecclesiam, incepto sonore a quodam
fratre Radulfo iuniore, 'Te Deum laudamus' et, pulsato classico,
laudes Deo exsoluimus in iubilo:

> Laudet omnis creatura   Creatorem omnium,
> Qui in crucis sue laudem   uere confitentium
> Corda mouet et compungit   ad amorem intimum,
>
> Qui ex atro silice[a]   terris inau|ditum
> Virtute potentie   instaurat miraculum,
> Huic laus atque gloria, honor atque uictoria Deo sit in secula.[3]

fo. 117ᵛ

xxix. *De discordia comitis Galfridi de Mandeuilla et Willelmi comitis de
Arundel.*

Seditionis tempore cum se inequaliter agerent homines in terra
nostra, et de pari contenderet modicus cum magno, humilis cum
summo, et fide penitus subacta, nullo respectu habito serui ad
dominum,[4] sic uacillaret regnum et regni status miserabili ductore[5]
premeretur fere usque ad exinanicionem,[b] e uicino contendebant
intra se duo de precipuis terre baronibus, Gaufridus de Mandeuille et Comes de Harundel,[6] quem post decessum regis Henrici
coniugio regine Adelidis contigit honorari, unde et superbire et
supra se extolli cepit ultra modum ut non[c] posset sibi pati parem,

---

[a] salice *H*   [b] exinatutionem *C*   [c] non *later interlinear addition in C*

---

[1] As the author was still a boy, this event could hardly be later than *c.* 1130.
[2] One of his duties as an acolyte; see above, p. xxxi.
[3] This hymn is not apparently attested elsewhere (it is not listed in H. Walther, *Initia Carminum ac Versuum Medii Aevi Posterioris Latinorum* (Göttingen, 1959)). It is made up of stanzas in various rhythms. The first three lines are 8p + 7pp (in the notation of D. Norberg, *Introduction à l'étude de la versification latine médiévale* (Stockholm, 1958), in which the first eight syllables bear stress on the paroxytone (p) or penultimate syllable— 8p—with the remaining seven syllables being stressed on the proparoxytone (pp) or antepenultimate syllable—7pp, whence the rhythm of the entire line is 8p + 7pp). The following two verses ('Qui ex atro . . . miraculum') are 7pp + 7pp, although as preserved the second half of the first line is a syllable short; the deficiency could be rectified by supplying a monosyllabic word such as *nunc*: 'terris ⟨nunc⟩ inauditum'. The final line ('Huic laus . . . in secula') is not rhythmical verse as preserved; however, if the trans-

overjoyed. I was a boy at the time,[1] and on duty for the week with other boys as censer.[2] One moment I was weeping, at another laughing, apeing the other boys.

When we reached the church the singing of the 'Te Deum laudamus' had been begun by one of the brethren called Ralph the Younger; the bells were rung, and we expressed our praises to God in a hymn of praise:

Let every creature praise the Creator of all,
    Who stirs the hearts of the truly faithful
To praise His Cross, and spurs them
    To even deeper love.
To God who by His excellent power
    Wrought from black stone a miracle unheard of on earth,
To Him be praise and glory, honour and victory
    For evermore.[3]

29. *The quarrel between Earl Geoffrey de Mandeville and William, earl of Arundel.*

At the time of the civil discord when men in our land were behaving without concern for right order, ordinary men vied with the great, men of low estate with those in high position, loyalty was utterly abandoned and servants had no respect for their masters.[4] Hence, the kingdom tottered and its stability was assailed almost to the point of destruction by a pitiable leader.[5] It was then that two of the leading barons in the land, Geoffrey de Mandeville and the earl of Arundel,[6] fought with each other from their neighbouring lands. After the death of King Henry it was the earl of Arundel's good fortune to have the honour of marrying Queen Adeliza. As a result he became arrogant and inordinately conceited so that he could not bear anyone being his equal, and anything that our world

mitted *atque* is replaced on each occasion by *et*, the line will consist of three elements of 7pp: 'Huic laus et glória / honor et uictória / Deo sit in sécula.'
  We are very grateful to Michael Lapidge for supplying the information in this note.
  [4] A reference to the disorders of Stephen's reign.
  [5] Almost certainly King Stephen; the author, who owed his prebend to Queen Adeliza, Henry I's widow, would have had no difficulty in attaching blame for the disorders to the man who deprived her of her dower in Waltham.
  [6] William d'Aubigny acquired the castle of Arundel after his marriage to Queen Adeliza in 1138, and was made earl of Arundel (sometimes called 'of Sussex') not later than 1141 (*Complete Peerage*, i. 233–5; R. H. C. Davis, *King Stephen* (3rd edn., London, 1990), pp. 135–6).

fo. 118ʳ et uilesceret in oculis eius quicquid pre|cipuum preter regem in se habebat noster mundus.

Habebat tunc temporis Willelmus ille, pincerna,[1] nondum comes, dotem regine[2] Waltham contiguam terris comitis Gaufridi de Mandeuille,[3] inpatiens quidem omnium comprouintialium terras suo dominio non mancipari. E contra Gaufridus iste precellens multiformi gratia, precipuus totius Anglie, militia quidem precliuis, morum uenustate preclarus, in consiliis regiis et regni moderamine cunctis preminens, agebat se inter ceteros quasi unus ex illis, nullius probitatis sue garrulus, nullius probitatis sibi collate uel dignitatis nimius ostentator, rei sue familiaris prouidus dispensator, omnium uirtutum communium que tantum decerent uirum affluentia exuberans si Dei gratiam diligentius acceptam et

fo. 118ᵛ ceteris prelatam diligens executor menti sue | sedulus imprimeret. Nouit populus quod non mentior, quem si laudibus extulerim meritis eius assignari potius quam gratie nostre id debere credimus, uerunptamen gratie diuine de cuius munere uenit quicquid boni prouenit homini.[4]

xxx. *Qualiter Galfridus comes de Mandeuilla succendit uillam de Waltham, et crux sancta deponitur. Comes uulneratur et moritur.*

Intra se igitur tanti uiri pacis et tranquillitatis metas excedentes et seditiose alter alterius predia uastantes, contigit Gaufridum, furore exagitatum quia succenderat Willelmus domos suas[5] et uniuersam predam terre sue abigi fecerat, uillam Walthamensem succendere, nec posse domibus canonicorum parcere que reliquis domibus erant contigue; testimonium perhibemus qui et dampna cum ceteris sustinuimus:[6] unde requisitus cum nollet satisfacere,

---

[1] William d'Aubigny, like his father, was *pincerna regis*. Royal butlers were household officers of some dignity; but here the author, who was clearly hostile to d'Aubigny, contrasts his status with that of an earl, as if to imply that he was something of an upstart.

[2] Waltham, as queen's dower, was in fact given by Stephen to his wife, Queen Matilda, in 1141; the Empress Matilda was able to restore it, briefly at least, to Adeliza (Ransford, *Waltham Charters*, nos. 19, 21; *Regesta* iii, nos. 915, 918).

[3] The Mandeville estate included Enfield, Edmonton, and South Mimms down to the late 12th cent., so that Geoffrey's property adjoined William's at Waltham; see *VCH Middlesex*, v. 149, 224, 282.

[4] The author gives one of the few favourable contemporary assessments of Geoffrey's character; for the most recent assessments of the period, see *The Anarchy of Stephen's Reign*, ed. Edmund King (Oxford, forthcoming).

[5] Geoffrey held manors in Sawbridgeworth, Saffron Walden, and Great Waltham,

possessed that was special, apart from the king, was worthless in his eyes.

At that time this William, who was a butler[1] and not yet an earl, gained Waltham as the dowry of the queen.[2] This adjoined the lands of Geoffrey de Mandeville,[3] but William could not endure it unless the lands of all who lived in the same district as he were surrendered to his estate. In contrast Geoffrey surpassed all men in every estimable quality. He was one of the most eminent men in the whole of England, distinguished in arms, a man of exceptional qualities, pre-eminent over all other men in the counsels of the king and in the government of the realm, but behaving amongst other men as one of them. He did not brag of any goodness, nor make a show of displaying it or the power that had been conferred upon him. He was a wise steward of his own property, and abounded in all the common virtues which so befit a man of wealth when, as a careful and industrious administrator, he has implanted in his own mind an awareness of the grace of God which has been earnestly received and cherished above all else. The people know that I do not lie, and if I have praised that man highly I believe that this should be attributed to his merit rather than to any favour of mine, or rather, to God's grace, for whatever good happens to a man comes to him as a gift from God.[4]

30. *Geoffrey de Mandeville sets fire to the vill of Waltham, and the holy cross is taken down. The earl is wounded and dies.*

Between them, therefore, these powerful men overstepped the bounds of peace and tranquillity, and seditiously devastated each other's estates. What happened was that Geoffrey was roused to a fury because William had set fire to his houses[5] and had everything which he had plundered removed to his own land. Geoffrey therefore set fire to the vill of Waltham, but was not able to spare the houses of the canons which adjoined the other houses. I can bear witness to this since I sustained the same loss as the others.[6] When Geoffrey, on being requested to compensate them, refused to do

and the reference may be to houses in any of these. The date of these events is probably some time after Stephen's condemnation of Geoffrey in the autumn of 1143, when d'Aubigny may have considered that he was obeying the king's orders.

[6] The author, who was then about twenty-four or twenty-five, was evidently a canon with a house of his own; this may indicate that he was married.

placuit fratribus ibidem Deo seruientibus, in transgressionis huius
uin|dictam, crucem deponere si forte diues ille compunctus hoc
facto uellet resipiscere.¹ Tradunt autem qui hiis inquirendis dili-
gentiam adibuerunt, eadem depositionis hora, comitem illum ante
castrum de Burewelle, ad quod expugnandum diligenter operam
dabat, letale uulnus suscepisse, et eo infra .xl. dies uiam uniuerse
carnis ingressum fuisse.²

xxxi. *De quinque Flandrensibus spoliantibus ecclesiam tempore incendii et
non ualentibus egredi.*

Tempore igitur incendii supramemorati, dum obseruaret comes
ille ecclesiam cum multis ne succenderetur, amicissimus ipse et
deuotus ecclesie, afflictus multo dolore quod periclitarentur res
ecclesie, non tamen poterat manentibus illis iniuriam sibi illatam
uindicare; contigit quiddam dictu mirabile, nam quidam satellites
de suis, ipso nesciente, quinque Flandrenses³ filii Belial⁴ | eccle-
siam ingressi, sarcinulas deportatas ad ecclesiam ob pacis et rerum
conseruandarum remedium arriperent, ad asportandas eas hostia
ecclesie laborando queritarent set obstante crucis signo nec ecclesiam exire nec sarcinulas transferre permissi sunt donec sedatis
omnibus et sublatis de medio aduersariis pax data est uille; et
reuersi iam nostri qui insecuti fuerant gentem aduersam, intrantes
ecclesiam ut sarcinulas suas reportarent ad propria,⁵ inuenerunt
filios Belial circumuagantes per semitas ubi patebat eis uia, nam
plena erat cistis et armariis propter hanc seditionem ecclesia,
adhuc deportantes sarcinulas; quos cum comprehendissent nostri
furore exagitati, dum uellent a sanctuario expellere, obstitit
Warmundus sacrista uir bonus, uite laudabilis et Deo deuotus; et

---

¹ An example of the common practice of 'humiliation of the saints': a ritual laying of
relics or crosses on the ground, sometimes surrounded with thorns, in protest at acts of
violence and desecration; they might be left there until reparation had been made. See
Patrick Geary, 'L'humiliation des saints', *Annales*, xxxiv (1979), 27–42.
² Geoffrey de Mandeville was mortally wounded while besieging Burwell, and died
on 16 September 1144 (*Monasticon* iv. 140; *Gesta Stephani*, p. 166). William of Newburgh
(i. 46) said he died a few days after being wounded.
³ An important element in Stephen's army consisted of Flemish mercenaries led by
William of Ypres. Flemish knights were also hired by the Empress Matilda, and
evidently also by some individual magnates, since the five men who violated the
sanctuary at Waltham are said to have been de Mandeville's retainers.
⁴ The name Belial, used in the Old Testament as an evil or worthless person, came to

so, the brethren who served God in that place decided, as a punishment for his sins, to take down the cross in the hope that that wealthy man would be pricked in his conscience by this action, and would be willing to reconsider.[1] Those who have made a careful investigation of these events have recorded that at the very hour the cross was taken down the earl received a mortal wound outside the castle of Burwell which he was assiduously attacking, and within forty days he had gone the way of all flesh.[2]

31. *Five men of Flanders rob the church at the time of the fire, and are power-less to leave the building.*

At the time of the fire related above Earl Geoffrey was keeping watch on the church with many of his men to see that it was not set on fire, for he was himself a good friend of the church and devoted to it. He was very concerned that they might be endangering church property, yet he was unable to avenge the wrong inflicted upon himself without damaging it. Then something happened which is marvellous to relate. Five Fleming retainers of his,[3] being sons of Belial,[4] entered the church without the earl's knowledge, and stole bundles which had been brought to the church for peaceful protection and the preservation of property; but they had great difficulty when searching for the doors of the church in carrying out the bundles, for the image of the cross stood in their way, and they were not allowed to leave the church and remove the packages until everything had been restored to order, the antagonists had been removed from the district, and peace restored to the town. Our men, returning now from pursuing the foe, on entering the church to restore their packages to their proper owners,[5] found these children of Belial still carrying them, wandering along passages wherever a way was open to them, for the church was full of boxes and chests because of this time of civil strife. When our men arrested them, being stirred to a fury they wanted to drive them out of that place of sanctuary, but the sacristan Warmund, a good and virtuous man who was a devoted servant of God, stopped

be used (as by Paul, 2 Cor. 6: 15) of the antagonist of God. 'Sons of Belial' passed into popular speech for evil-doers.
[5] For the use of churches to store valuables in times of war, see above, p. xxxii.

fo. 120^r utroque lumine priuatos, cecos quidem oculorum et cordis | acie
^aduxit ante altare et compunctos corde, erat enim eis necesse,
diutissime flagris cesos, reddita^a eis sanitate miseratione diuina,
conduxit per uillam, multis obstare uolentibus, set reuerentiam
exibentes conductori, liberos dimiserunt filios diaboli.

xxxii. *De Hunfrido Barentune furioso, et de equo suo, tempore incendii.*

Eadem die uir quidam nomine Hunfridus de Barentone,[1] per
manum domini Gileberti de Munfichet forestarius in prouintia,
ueniens cum reliquis spiritu nequam debriatis, equo sedens
intrauit ecclesiam ut satellitibus Belial precepta daret, pronos ad
malum ad deteriora animaret: a domo Dei equum insidens exiuit;
complices suos insequens ad compitum extra burgum uenit ubi
correpti a demonio et ipse et cui insidebat equus pene transgres-
fo. 120^v sionis et uesanie sue susceper|at talionem; equus namque inibi a
diabolo suffocatus est, miles in ecclesiam multorum manibus, quia
uicinus noster erat, deportatus, uix triduo fusa frequenti oratione
pro illo restitutus est sanitati.

In retributionem itaque collati sibi a domino benefitii prefatus
miles ecclesie contulit in memoriale donum .xiiii. acras terre[2] cum
prato adiacenti iuxta dominium cuiusdam prebende in Luchen-
tuna.

xxxiii. *Qualiter Robertus aurifaber et plures canonici percussi sunt cecitate
cum laminam femoralem subleuarent.*

Eadem igitur temporis statione cum humiliata terre iaceret crux
nostra, consilio capituli selecti^b sunt duo de fratribus, Robertus
filius Walteri et Adam filius Bruningi,[3] qui sedulam darent operam

^{a–a} duxit ante altare, erat enim necesse, diutissime flagris cesos, ueniam Dei implor-
are compunctos corde, reddita *H*   ^b se electi *C*; electi *H*

---

[1] Humphrey of Barrington was a local forester under Gilbert of (Stansted) Mountfitchet. He was a supporter of Geoffrey de Mandeville: a charter of Geoffrey confirms
land jointly to Eustace and his son Humphrey (G. Allan Lowndes, 'The history of the
Barrington family', *TEAS*, new ser., i (1878), 251–73, at p. 253).
[2] In some charters confirming the possessions of the canons, Humphrey is mentioned as a benefactor ('terram quam dedit Hunfred de Barenton ipsi ecclesie de
Waltham', Ransford, *Waltham Charters*, nos. 26, 28–30); this seems to be a confirmation
of the gift mentioned here.

them from doing this. He led these men, who had been deprived of their sight in both eyes and were as blind in heart as they were in sight, straight to the altar, and pricked in their consciences, as they inevitably were, they received a sound whipping. When their sight had been restored to them by God's mercy, Warmund led them through the vill, though many wanted to stop him, but showing reverence for the guide they let these sons of the devil go free.

32. *The story of the mad Humphrey of Barrington and his horse at the time of the fire.*

On the same day a man called Humphrey of Barrington,[1] a forester in the shire in the service of Lord Gilbert of Mountfitchet, came with other men possessed of an evil spirit and entered the church on horseback. He was intent on giving orders to those followers of Belial, and of stirring to even worse acts men who were of sinful inclination. Then he left God's house astride his horse; following his accomplices he came to the crossroads outside the town where both he, and the horse upon which he was sitting, were seized by a demon, and he almost suffered the penalty for his sin and madness. Indeed, his horse was there and then choked by the devil, but the knight was carried into the church in the hands of many people, for he was a neighbour of ours. After barely three days of constant prayer on his behalf he was restored to his right mind.

As a recompense for the kindness shown him by the Lord this knight conferred upon the church in perpetuity a gift of fourteen acres of land[2] with adjoining meadowland next to the estate of a certain prebend at Loughton.

33. *Robert the goldsmith and several canons were struck with blindness when they raised the femoral plate.*

At the same period of time, when our cross was lying humiliated upon the ground, two of our brethren, Robert son of Walter and Adam son of Bruning,[3] were selected by decision of the chapter to

---

[3] Adam was the son of an earlier canon and priest, Bruning, who died *c.* 1115 × 1118 (Ransford, *Waltham Charters*, nos. 11, 13); his position is evidence of the tendency of the prebends to become hereditary.

in ueteranis laminis[2] et erugine obductis crucifixi ut mundarentur
et burnirentur[1] que uetustate ipsa oboleuerant; lapides etiam
fo. 121ʳ preciosi qui circulis suis[3] uetustate consumptis | ceciderant pris-
tinis locis restituerentur. Factum est, dum obseruarent aurifabros
ne malignandi daretur eis copia, cum subleuasset Robertus, aurifaber Sancti Albani, laminam auream femoralem ut priuaretur ipse
omni lumine et manuum operationis aminiculo, et offitio occu-
lorum suspensi sunt predicti duo canonici et Warmundus sacrista
et Antonius custos ecclesie et Alwinus Bisemare carpentarius,
Edmundus dormitorii custos[4] et duo seruientes aurifabri, et ita
manerent stupidi non uidentes ab hora tertia usque ad uesper-
tinale offitium; set cum sero uouissent[a] se nunquam manus apposi-
turos amplius, respectu miserationis diuine lumen amissum
receperunt, ulterius huic sanctuario manus immundas non[b] appli-
caturi.[5]

---

[a] nouissent *H*   [b] *om. H*

---

[1] This is an earlier attestation of the use of *burnire* than any in *DMLBS*.
[2] For the ancient plating, see above, pp. 20–1 and n. 1.
[3] The girdle had been given by Tovi's wife Gytha; see above, cap. 13.
[4] Although the canons had their own houses in the town it is possible that some slept
in turn in the dormitory; alternatively it may have been used by the boys. For the *custos
dormitorii*, see above, p. xxxii.

give diligent attention to cleaning and burnishing[1] the ancient plating[2] of the crucifix which was tarnished and had decayed because of its very age. The precious stones which had fallen out of its girdle,[3] now worn with age, were to be restored to their former setting. It happened that while they were watching the goldsmiths to see that no opportunity was afforded them of harming it, Robert, the goldsmith of St Albans, raised the gold-plate around the thigh with the result that he lost the sight of his eyes and the power of using his hands. Sight was also withheld from the eyes of the two canons I have mentioned as well as from the sacristan Warmund, Anthony the custodian of the church, Alwin Bisemar the carpenter, Edmund warden of the dormitory,[4] and from two assistant goldsmiths. They all remained stunned and without sight from nine o'clock in the morning until the time of Vespers. However, when later they vowed that they would never lay their hands upon it in future, through God's mercy they recovered their lost sight, intending after this not to touch this holy relic with unclean hands.[5]

---

[5] The Chronicle ends here, with no concluding section. Possibly the intention was to add new miracles as they occurred; but it may have been incompletely copied.

APPENDIX I

York Minster Library, MS XVI. Q. 14, fo. 76v.[1]

L. Gualthamense solum doctis natale poetis
    militibusque probis, Petre, fuisse patet.
Nec puto turpe mihi natale solum profiteri,
    quo natura decus dat speciale sibi;
que pariens quid possit ibi studiosa probauit;
    uestiit et uario larga decore locum.
Nam quis humum, quis dulce nemus, quis prata decoris,
    quis digna uarias laude loquatur aquas?
Et licet ipse locum situs efferat aptus amenum,
    ars tamen accedens edibus ornat eum.
Has si conspiceret, puto, Dedalus ipse stuperet,
    artificisque manum disceret artis inops.
Ars operosa piros, oleam,[2] pomeria, uitem,
    ficum, castaneas, addidit atque nucem.
Esculus expansis et coctanus undique ramis,
    persicus et morus multa reludit ibi.
Cetera quid memorem? sterilis speciale iuuamen
    mandragoras uteri, Petre, silebo tibi.
Nec tibi pulchra loquar uiridaria, te nec in ortos
    inducam uarios.   P. Quos? olerumne? placet.
Allia uel cepas mihi parua uidere uoluptas,
    nedum quod stomacus noster abhorret holus.
L. Si quibus areolis, quo scemate curat, et ortos
    ars operalis eos qua ratione serit,
ordine quo plantat, uel qualibus irrigat undis,
    si tibi, Petre, loquar: sed quid ad ista morer?
Surgat, et ecclesiam Sancte Crucis arte stupendam
    noster sermo petat.   P. Pulcra sit: esto breuis.
L. Est formosa modum specialiter ipsa per omnem.
    Sumne breuis?   P. Breuitas effluit ista satis.
L. Cum sua forma sacram satis et super efferat edem,

---

[1] *DLD*, iii. 333–370, 435–440. Composed after 1128, these lines describe Waltham as Laurence had known it in his boyhood. See above, p. xxxi.
[2] Olives cannot have been cultivated at Waltham in the 12th cent. Although Laurence was not writing a fictional colloquy with a lexicographic rather than a descriptive intent, he may have been influenced by some lexicographic list to include a tree that did not

APPENDIX I

Laurence of Durham: Dialogi *iii. 333 – 370 and 435 – 440*[1]

LAURENCE. It is well known, Peter, that Waltham was the birthplace of learned poets and fine soldiers. And I do not think it wrong for me to speak of my birthplace where nature bestows special honour upon herself. In her zeal she thought it right to produce what she could and she bounteously clothed the place with all kinds of glorious things. For who can adequately praise its soil, pleasant woodland, beautiful meadows, and manifold streams! and though the situation itself is ideal for making the place delightful, yet man's art comes and adorns it with buildings. If Daedalus himself could see these I think he would be amazed and would recognize the hand of the artist and feel inadequate himself. The gardener's skill has added pear-trees, olives,[2] orchards, vines, fig-trees, chestnut-trees, and nut trees. The oak and the quince-tree are on all sides with their spreading branches, and peaches and mulberries rejoice there. Why need I say more? I will say nothing of the mandrakes, a special remedy for the barren womb, nor tell you of the beautiful plantation of trees or lead you into the varied gardens.

PETER. Which gardens? Do you mean vegetable gardens? If you must! But it will give me little pleasure to visualize garlic or onions, let alone cabbage, which my stomach hates.

LAURENCE. If I were to tell you, Peter, of the different kinds of beds and their arrangement in which the gardener tends these things and by what method he sows those gardens, the lines in which he plants and the sort of streams he uses to water them—but why do I linger over these things? Let my speech rise up and take as its subject the Church of the Holy Cross, amazing for its architecture.

PETER. It may be beautiful: but be brief.

LAURENCE. It is particularly beautiful in itself in every respect. Am I brief enough?

PETER. Such brevity is quite overwhelming!

LAURENCE. Since its own beauty exalts this holy church more than I can

grow in England. Cf. Patrizia Lendinara's comment on a *Colloquy* of Ælfric Bata, 'The lists of trees which are supposed to grow in the orchard of the monastery amount to some hundred different species and among the hunter's quarry there are animals which never belonged to the English fauna' ('The *Oratio de utensilibus ad domum regendam pertinentibus* by Adam of Balsham', *ANS* xv (1993), 162–76, at p. 172).

cetera quo taceam? clerus honorat eam;
clerus et auleis, multo plus clerus et auro,
 clerus et argento, clerus et ere suo;
clerus et innumeris plus hanc ornatibus ornat,
 illius iste domus uernat in omne decus.
Paruus ab his in ea paruo cum fratre, paterne
 nutritus, didici multa tenenda mihi.

· · · · · · · ·

L. Cum puer in iuuenem tener ire uiderer ephebum,
 cepi maturos uiuere uelle senes;
 et pariter natale solum, mihi uestis, et etas
 uertitur, in iuuenem uado repente puer;
 et laicum monacho Gualtham permuto Dunelmo,
 inque nouum penitus nitor abire uirum.

say, how can I be silent about other things? The clergy adorn it; they adorn it with tapestries, and much more so with gold, with silver, and with their own bronze. The clergy adorn it still more with innumerable adornments. Their temple itself is beauteous with all its glory. As a young boy, along with my small brother, I was brought up by these men in a fatherly way, and I learnt many things worth remembering.

. . . .

LAURENCE. When as a tender youth I felt I was reaching manhood, I began to desire a life amongst wise old men. So I moved from my birthplace; my clothing and my life altered, and suddenly I passed from childhood to manhood; I gave up 'secular' Waltham to become a monk at Durham, and I strove with all my heart to become a new man.

APPENDIX II[1]

Versus Circa Tumbam Haroldi Regis

Macte pater patrie, meritis insignis Harolde,
Parma, pugil, gladius: te tegit hic tumulus.
Qui cum rege truci[2] mundi subducere luci;
Classica non trepidas que uehit huc Boreas.
Omen at infaustum tua signa retorsit ad austrum,
Nam tua fata scies in noua bella ruens.

⟨In⟩ hoc mausoleo fortis requiescit Haroldus
qui fuit Anglorum gentis rex inclitus olim,
cui fauor imperium species natura potestas
contulit et regnum, dans cum dyademate sceptrum.
Dum pugil insignis proprias defendere gentes
nititur, occubuit Francorum gente peremptus.
Huius nobilibus successibus inuida fata
quem neqeunt saluare necant fraudemque sequuntur.

Item versus de aduentu sancte crucis et canonicorum secularium apud Waltham

Waltham ualle datur: habita cruce nobilitatur:
succreuitque chorus mundani canonicatus.
Martirium Thome memoratur religione.
Fundat et edificat, renouat rex, papaque firmat.
Eximitur: liberaque datur, sub eis dominatur
hic datus undique stas ut in ordine dignior abbas.

Item versus de libertate et dignitate canonicorum regularium

Quatuor utendis Waltham preerat simul istis:
Ordine, paupere rebus et hospite nomine cure.
Continuabatur antiquitus usus in illis,
Absit quod nouitas transgrediatur eas.

[1] British Library, Harley MS 3776, fos. 62ʳ and 62ᵛ. See above, p. li.

APPENDIX II[1]

Verses upon the tomb of King Harold

Blessed father of our country, Harold marked out by your merits,
You, our shield, fist, and sword: now a mound covers you,
Who, taken now from this world's light with that fierce king,[2]
Do not fear the trumpet's blasts issuing from the north.
An omen, but a bad one, turned your standards towards the south
That you might learn your fate when hastening into unknown wars.

In this tomb brave Harold rests
who once famed king of England was
on whom renown, mien, character and authority
conferred power and a kingdom, a sceptre and a crown as well.
Until he strove, a famed warrior, to defend his very own
people, but died, slain by the men of France.
The Fates, so envious of his noble conquests,
kill him they cannot save, and pursue deceit.

Likewise verses on the arrival of the Holy Cross and secular canons at Waltham

Waltham is granted them in the valley, ennobled by the Cross it holds:
a choir of Canons Secular grew up together here.
But now the martyrdom of Thomas is remembered here by monks.
A King founds, builds and renews the church and the pope confirms it.
It enjoys exemption, and is granted liberty; by both lords it is ruled.
An abbot, given here, holds sway, and everywhere, Waltham, you stand
    in greater honour.

Likewise verses about the freedom and high position of the regular canons

In these four things together Waltham excelled:
Order, the poor, the cure of souls and hospitality.
From of old the practice of these benefits has continued,
God forbid that they be neglected by the new Order.

[2] Harold Hardrada, king of Norway, killed by Harold at Stamford Bridge.

INDEX OF QUOTATIONS AND ALLUSIONS

A. BIBLICAL ALLUSIONS

B. CITATIONS FROM CLASSICAL AND MEDIEVAL SOURCES

GENERAL INDEX